MW01098495

Level D

Vocabulary

Isabel L. Beck, Ph.D. and
Margaret G. McKeown, Ph.D.

Read-Aloud Anthology

www.Steck-Vaughn.com
1-800-531-5015

Acknowledgments

Literature

Grateful acknowledgment is given to the following publishers and copyright owners for permissions granted to reprint selections from their publications. All possible care has been taken to trace ownership and secure permission for each selection included. In the case of any errors or omissions, the Publisher will be pleased to make suitable acknowledgments in future editions.

p. 1, "The Birthday of Madeleine Blore" by Karla Kuskin. Copyright © 1995 by Karla Kuskin. Used by permission of S©ott Treimel NY.

p. 9, Adapted from"In the Shower with Andy" from *Just Annoying!* by Andy Griffiths. Copyright © 1998 by Backyard Stories Pty Ltd. Reprinted by permission of Scholastic Inc. Illustration for "In the Shower with Andy" by Adam Stower from *More Funny Stories*. © 2003. Reproduced by permission of the publisher Kingfisher Publications plc. All rights reserved.

p. 28, "The Tour" from *It's Not About The Bike* by Lance Armstrong. Copyright © 2000 by Lance Armstrong. Used by permission of G.P. Putnam's Sons, a division of Penguin Group (USA) Inc.

p. 35, "The Marble Champ" from *Baseball in April and Other Stories* by Gary Soto. Copyright © 1990 by Gary Soto. Reprinted by permission of Harcourt, Inc.

p. 45, Excerpts from "Smith Wilkinson: The Same Thing Over and Over" and "Kid Blink and the Newsies: Bringing Down Goliaths" from *We Were There, Too!* by Phillip Hoose. Copyright © 2001 by Phillip Hoose. Reprinted by permission of Farrar, Straus and Giroux, LLC.

p. 53, "Macavity: The Mystery Cat" from *Old Possum's Book Of Practical Cats* by T.S. Eliot, illustrated by Edward Gorey. Text copyright © 1939 by T.S. Eliot and renewed 1967 by Esme Valerie Eliot. Illustration copyright © 1982 by Edward Gorey. Reprinted by permission of Harcourt, Inc.

p. 59, *Bigfoot Cinderrrrrella* by Tony Johnston, illustrated by James Warhola. Text copyright © 1998 by Tony Johnston. Illustrations copyright © 1998 by James Warhola. Used by permission of G.P. Putnam's Sons, a Division of Penguin Young Readers Group, a Member of Penguin Group (USA) Inc., 345 Hudson Street, New York, NY 10014. All rights reserved.

p. 69, "The President's Bumpy Ride" by Connie Nordhielm Wooldridge. Reprinted by permission of *Cricket Magazine*, July 2004. Copyright © 2004 by Connie Nordhielm Wooldridge.

p. 76, "Helping Hooves" by Michael Neill, Michaele Ballard/ People © 2001, Time Inc. All rights reserved.

p. 82, "Egged on by Pete" from *The Further Adventures of Hank the Cowdog* by John R. Erickson. Copyright © 1983 by John R. Erickson. Used by permission of Puffin Books, a Division of Penguin Young Readers Group, a Member of Penguin Group (USA) Inc., 345 Hudson Street, New York, NY 10014. All rights reserved.

p. 94, Text from "Space Rock Barely Misses Sleeping Teen" from *Current Science*, August 29, 2003, Vol. 89 Issue 1. Copyright 2003 Weekly Reader Corp. Reprinted with permission from WRC Media Inc. "Comet" by Ann Pedtke. Reprinted by permission of *Cricket Magazine*, January 2005. Copyright © 2005 by Carus Publishing Company.

p. 101, "Home Sweet, Soddie" by Flo Ota De Lange from *Elements Of Literature*, Second Course. Copyright © 2005 by Holt, Rinehart and Winston. Reprinted by permission of the publisher.

p. 108, "Mattresses" from *Tales from the Brothers Grimm and the Sisters Weird* by Vivian Vande Velde. Copyright © 1995 by Vivian Vande Velde. Reprinted by permission of Harcourt, Inc.

p. 118, "A Day's Wait" from *The Short Stories of Ernest Hemingway*. Copyright 1933 Charles Scribner's Sons. Copyright renewed © 1961 by Mary Hemingway. Reprinted with permission of Scribner, an imprint of Simon & Schuster Adult Publishing Group.

p. 126, "The Merchant's Camel" by Amy Friedman from *Tell Me A Story*. © 1993 by Amy Friedman. Reprinted with permission of Andrews McMeel Publishing. All rights reserved.

p. 134, "Skeleton, in the flesh, is a real thrill" retitled "Skeleton Barrels Back into Olympics" by Mark Sappenfield. Reproduced with permission from the February 20, 2002 issue of The Christian Science Monitor (www.csmonitor.com). © 2002 The Christian Science Monitor. All rights reserved.

p. 141, "The Miller's Good Luck" from *My Land Sings: Stories from the Rio Grande* by Rudolph Anaya. Text copyright © 1999 by Rudolph Anaya. Used by permission of HarperCollins Publishers.

p. 153, "The World's Most Traveled Dog" by Richard Bauman. Reprinted by permission of *Cricket Magazine*, April 2005. Copyright © 2005 by Richard Bauman.

p. 178, "Flying With a Purpose" excerpted from *Bessie Coleman: First Black Woman Pilot*. © 2001 by Connie Plantz. Published by Enslow Publishers, Inc., Berkeley Heights, NJ. All rights reserved.

p. 185, *The Wise Old Woman* by Yoshiko Uchida. Courtesy of the Bancroft Library, University of California, Berkeley.

p. 195, *The Lion, The Witch and the Wardrobe* by C.S. Lewis. Copyright © C.S. Lewis Pte. Ltd. 1950. Illustrations by Pauline Baynes. Copyright © C.S. Lewis Pte. Ltd. 1950. Reprinted by permission.

Illustration

Lyuba Bogan pp. 1–8; Jennifer Emery pp. 22–27; Laurie Harden pp. 35–44; Nancy Harrison, pp. 69–74; Kimberly Bulcken Root pp. 82–93; Jeffrey Lindbergh pp. 94–100; Ron Himler pp. 101–105; Bradley Slocum pp. 108–115, 117; Ron Mazellan pp. 118–125; Robert Crawford pp. 141–152; Raphael Montoliu pp. 153–160; Steve Cieslawski pp. 161–167; Matthew Archambault pp. 168–175, 177; Carol Inouye pp. 185–194.

Photography

p. 28 © Ezra Shaw/Getty Images; p. 34 © Doug Pensinger/ Getty Images; pp. 46, 52, 75, 107 Courtesy of the Library of Congress; pp. 77, 80 © Todd Sumlin/The Charlotte Observer; p. 135 © Chris Trotman/CORBIS; p. 140 © Henry Ray Abrams/Getty Images; p. 179 Courtesy of the Miriam Matthews Collection; p. 184 © Bettmann/CORBIS. Additional photography by Photodisc/Getty Royalty Free.

ISBN 1-4190-3052-3

Printed in China 1 2 3 4 5 6 7 8 9 10 985 09 08 07 06

Contents

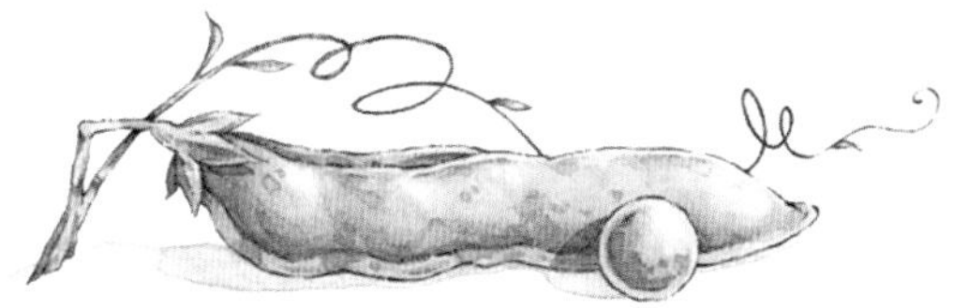

Research Says...

"Read quality literature to students to build a sense of story and to develop vocabulary and comprehension."

—National Reading Panel

The Magic of Reading Aloud

Many literate adults have fond memories of being read to as children. This is no coincidence. Reading research has shown that, besides being an enjoyable experience, reading aloud to children is a valuable tool in the teaching of language.

How Reading Aloud Fosters Vocabulary Development

Children begin understanding a variety of words long before they can read them. A word that could provide a stumbling block to a child reading silently is perfectly comprehensible when the child hears the word spoken and used in context. It follows, then, that a Read-Aloud Anthology is the perfect springboard for vocabulary development.

What This Read-Aloud Does	What This Means for You
Exposes children to rich, sophisticated words used in captivating, age-appropriate literature selections.	You can add a large store of descriptive, robust words and concepts to children's vocabularies.
Provides engaging vocabulary introduction strategies after each read-aloud.	You can introduce the vocabulary words in natural and memorable ways as part of your read-aloud discussion.
Encourages children to relate each vocabulary word to their own experiences.	You can help children make connections with powerful words—and enjoy hearing them make the words their own!

Bringing the *Story to Life*

There you are at center stage! Who, you? A performer? Yes! Just look at your audience, eagerly waiting for you to read them a story. Following some simple tips will help dramatize the performance and make it even more satisfying and valuable for children.

Tips for Reading Aloud

Practice reading ahead of time. Reading stories and poems aloud before reading to children helps you read fluently, with appropriate intonation and expression.

Introduce the story. Before you begin reading, show children the illustrations and ask what they think the story will be about.

Build background. If you think there are concepts in the selection that will be unfamiliar, provide enough background to help children understand the reading.

Read expressively. It's difficult to overdramatize when reading to children. Don't be afraid to use plenty of expression to reflect the mood of what you are reading.

Read slowly and clearly. Listeners will be better able to absorb and comprehend what you are saying when they have enough time to form mental images as they listen.

Pace your reading. The best pace is one that fits the story events. If exciting action is taking place, speed up a bit. To build suspense, slow down and lower your voice.

Use props. Bring in or make simple props if they will help clarify or enhance the story.

Involve your listeners. Encourage children to make sound effects or to provide rhyming or repeated words when a pattern has been established.

Ask questions. As you read, ask questions that allow listeners to make connections with their own experiences and stay engaged.

Listen as you read. Pay attention to children's comments during the story so you can build on those ideas and experiences in discussions after reading.

Enjoy yourself! If you are enthusiastic about what you are reading, children will learn that reading is an enjoyable activity.

Research Says...

...regular reading aloud strengthens children's reading, writing, and speaking skills—and thus the entire civilizing process.

—*The New Read-Aloud Handbook,* Jim Trelease

The Birthday of Madeleine Blore

A playful and rhythmic narrative poem, *The Birthday of Madeleine Blore* tells the story of Madeleine's exciting ninth birthday party and the mysterious gift that she has been waiting for all her life.

Vocabulary

Words From the Poem

These words appear in blue in the poem. Explain these words after the poem is read.

triumph **dazzle**
divine **vanish**

Words About the Poem

Explain these words after the poem is read, using context from the poem.

stupefy **dejected**
crave **fulfill**

Getting Ready for the Read-Aloud

Show students the picture of Madeleine's birthday party on pages 2–3. Read the title aloud. Explain that Madeleine is hoping to get a very special present for her birthday, a present that she has wanted for a long time. Point out the eager expression on Madeleine's face and the unique wrapping paper of the gift she is about to open.

Explain that this poem takes place during a girl's birthday party and is told from the point of view of one of the friends at the party. Have students talk about the best gift they've ever received, or a present they've wanted for a long time. You might want to have students guess what the present is.

The Birthday of Madeleine Blore

By Karla Kuskin
Illustrated by Lyuba Bogan

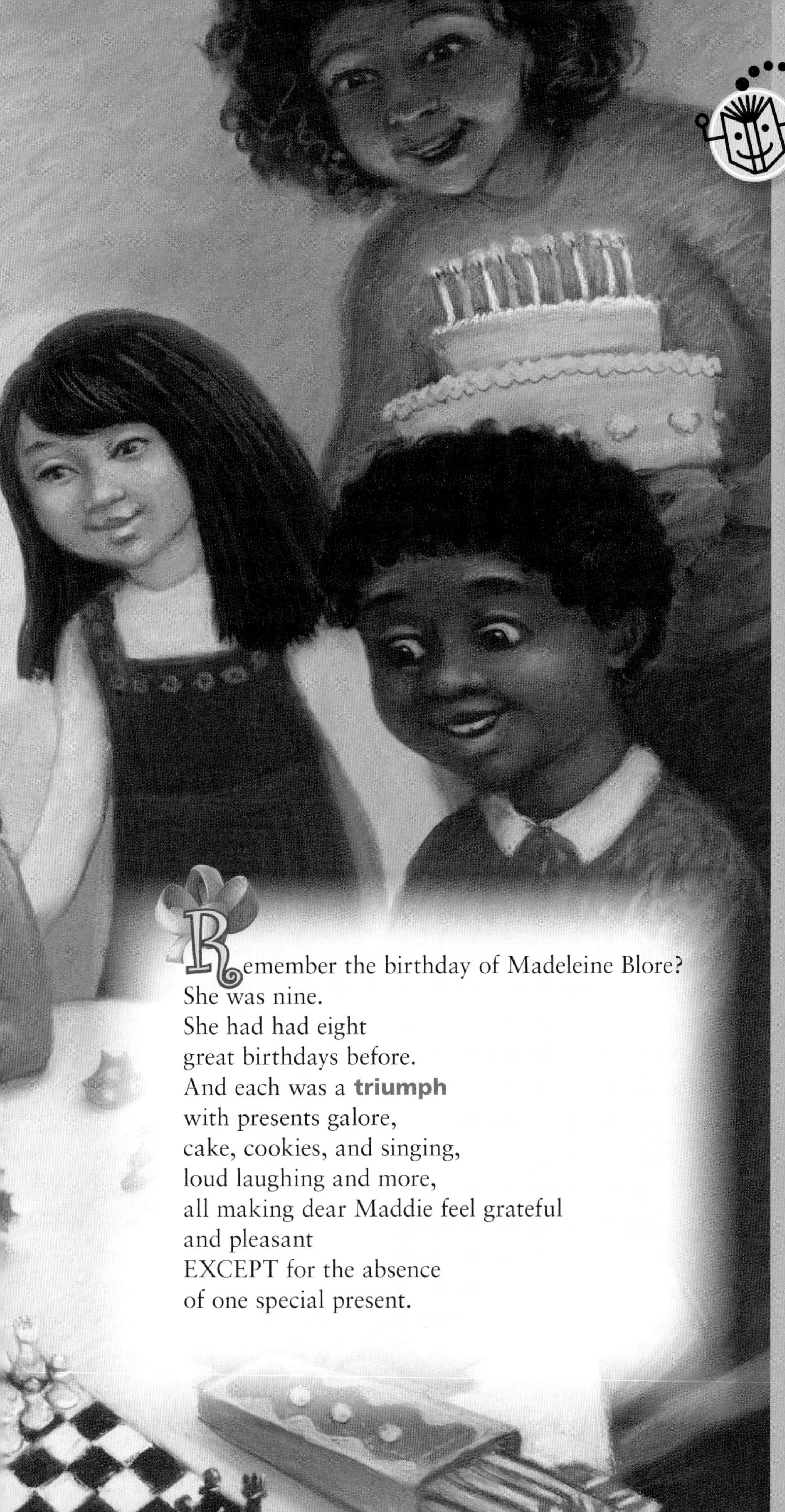

Remember the birthday of Madeleine Blore?
She was nine.
She had had eight
great birthdays before.
And each was a **triumph**
with presents galore,
cake, cookies, and singing,
loud laughing and more,
all making dear Maddie feel grateful
and pleasant
EXCEPT for the absence
of one special present.

Bringing the Poem to Life

Accentuate the poem's clear, playful rhythm. Make your reading tone that of a child at a birthday party: excited and anticipating. As you read, act out some of the actions in the poem, such as whispering, wiping a tear from your cheek, and rapping on a desk for the sound of a knock at the door. This poem lends itself well to a dramatic reading, especially with the surprises at the end.

What *was* it?
What was it?
Well what *could* it be?

What do you think the special present is?

If you asked,
there was silence from Madeleine B.
She only would say
that her birthdays were fine.
One through seven were heaven.
Eight was **divine**.
And now she was thrilled,
simply thrilled,
to be nine.

But then in a whisper
that no one could hear,
she would add, "Oh, if only
that present were here,"
as she brushed from her cheek
a small, sparkling tear.

Do you think the present will arrive during this party?

On the day of this birthday of Madeleine Blore,
a package arrived at a little past four.
First a ring of the bell,
then a rap at the door
and the next thing we knew
it was there
on the floor.
There was something about it—
the paper?
the size?
that filled us with wonder
and **dazzled** our eyes.
It was bigger than bigger
than bigger by half.

Did it hold a small house
or a little giraffe?
And the wrapping was special,
it looked to my eye as if it was wrapped
in a piece of the sky.

First Madeleine opened a puzzle from Jess,
then a bracelet from Jool,
then a sweet set of chess.
She loved every gift
and she thanked every giver.
The arrows were perfect, she said,
with the quiver.
She admired the old-fashioned
miniature store
and at last she approached
the big box on the floor.

She took off the paper
and opened the lid
and the strangest thing happened
as soon as she did.
When she opened the lid
and she peered deep inside,
her very brown eyes opened up very wide
and all of us leaned in to see what was there.

Now what do you think is in the package?

But there wasn't a thing
except empty-box air.

Madeleine smiled her most magical smile.
She took a deep breath
and she held it awhile.
And then with the teeniest, tiniest shout,
she reached in
and pulled all the emptiness out.
And she hugged it,
this nothing that no one could see
(except for the nine-year-old
Madeleine B.).

"Just look at the shape," she cried,
"look at the drape.
It is finally mine,
AN INVISIBLE CAPE.
Isn't it marvelous?
Isn't it clever?
It's just what I've wanted
for ever
and ever."

What do you think Madeleine will do with an invisible cape?

THEN
in less than a second,
or possibly two,
she wrapped the cape 'round her . . .

and **vanished** from view.

Talking About the Poem

Have students summarize what happened at the birthday party. Ask students whether or not they were surprised by the end of the poem.

Ask students what they thought of Madeleine Blore wanting an invisible cape. Ask students if they would want one?

Vocabulary in Action

Words From the Poem

triumph

In the poem, each of Madeleine's past birthday parties is described as a triumph. Something that is a triumph is a great success or achievement.

- Ask which event is a triumph, winning a sports game or losing a school election. Explain your answer.
- Have students put triumphant expressions on their faces.

divine

Madeleine's last birthday party was divine. If you call something divine, you are saying it is so wonderful it seems to come from out of this world.

- Ask which is divine, a car horn honking or some beautiful music. Why?
- Have students tell about a divine experience they have had.

dazzle

In the poem, Madeleine's mysterious package dazzled the other children's eyes. Something that dazzles you is so bright or so beautiful that it makes it hard to see.

- Ask students which image is dazzling, the sun shining on snow or a dark room. Why do you think so?
- Have students suggest other things that are dazzling.

vanish

Madeleine vanished when she put on the invisible cape. If someone or something vanishes, they disappear suddenly in a way that can't be explained.

- Ask students which has vanished, the shoe they're sure they tossed under the bed but which isn't there now or the puppy that's hiding in its doghouse. Why?
- Have students come up with ways to make their hands, fingers, or feet vanish from view.

Vocabulary in Action

Words About the Poem

stupefy

The children at the party were probably very surprised that the big package looked empty. Another way of saying somebody is very surprised is to say they were stupefied. If something stupefies you, it surprises you so much that it's hard to think.

- Ask which person is stupefied, the one who can't believe a movie ended the way it did even if the credits are rolling or the one who's listening to their favorite song on the radio. Explain.
- Ask students if they have ever stupefied someone. How?

crave

Madeleine wanted the invisible cape more than any other gift. You could also say that she craved the invisible cape. If you crave something, you want it so much you can hardly think of anything else.

- Ask who is craving food, the girl who just ate a nice, large dinner or the girl who's really hungry and waiting for dinner to be served. Explain why.
- Have students talk about what they crave right now.

dejected

At the end of her other birthday parties, Madeleine felt sad because she didn't get the gift she really wanted. You could also say Madeleine felt dejected. When you are dejected, you feel sad because you've been disappointed by something.

- Ask who would feel dejected, a boy going on vacation or a boy who is told that he can't go on vacation after all. Why do you think so?
- Have students pretend to be dejected.

fulfill

When Madeleine opened the package and found the invisible cape, her wish came true. Another way of saying that is that her wish was fulfilled. When a wish, dream, or hope is fulfilled, it comes true.

- Ask students which thing they would want fulfilled, a nice promise or a scary threat. Explain.
- Have students talk about dreams or wishes they would like to have fulfilled.

In the Shower with Andy

This humorous story tells what happens when a boy decides to fill up his shower cubicle with water by sealing it with his dad's caulk gun.

Vocabulary

Words From the Story

These words appear in blue in the story. Explain these words after the story is read.

cubicle **expel**
bail **abandon**
reinforce

Words About the Story

Explain these words after the story is read, using context from the story.

impetuous **resolutely**
dilemma

Getting Ready for the Read-Aloud

Show students the picture of Andy on page 10 and read the title aloud. Explain that Andy had thought it would be fun to seal up his shower and fill it with water. Have students notice that Andy doesn't look too happy about the situation he has created for himself.

Explain to students that this story takes place primarily in a shower. Then describe to them a caulk gun: a tool that pumps out a gooey, rubbery substance called caulk, which is used to seal cracks. You may also want to mention that the story is set in Australia.

There are some words and phrases in the story that may be new to students. You might wish to briefly explain these words and phrases as you come to them: *tap,* faucet; *insulation,* fluffy material in walls and attics that helps keep a home warm in the winter and cool in the summer.

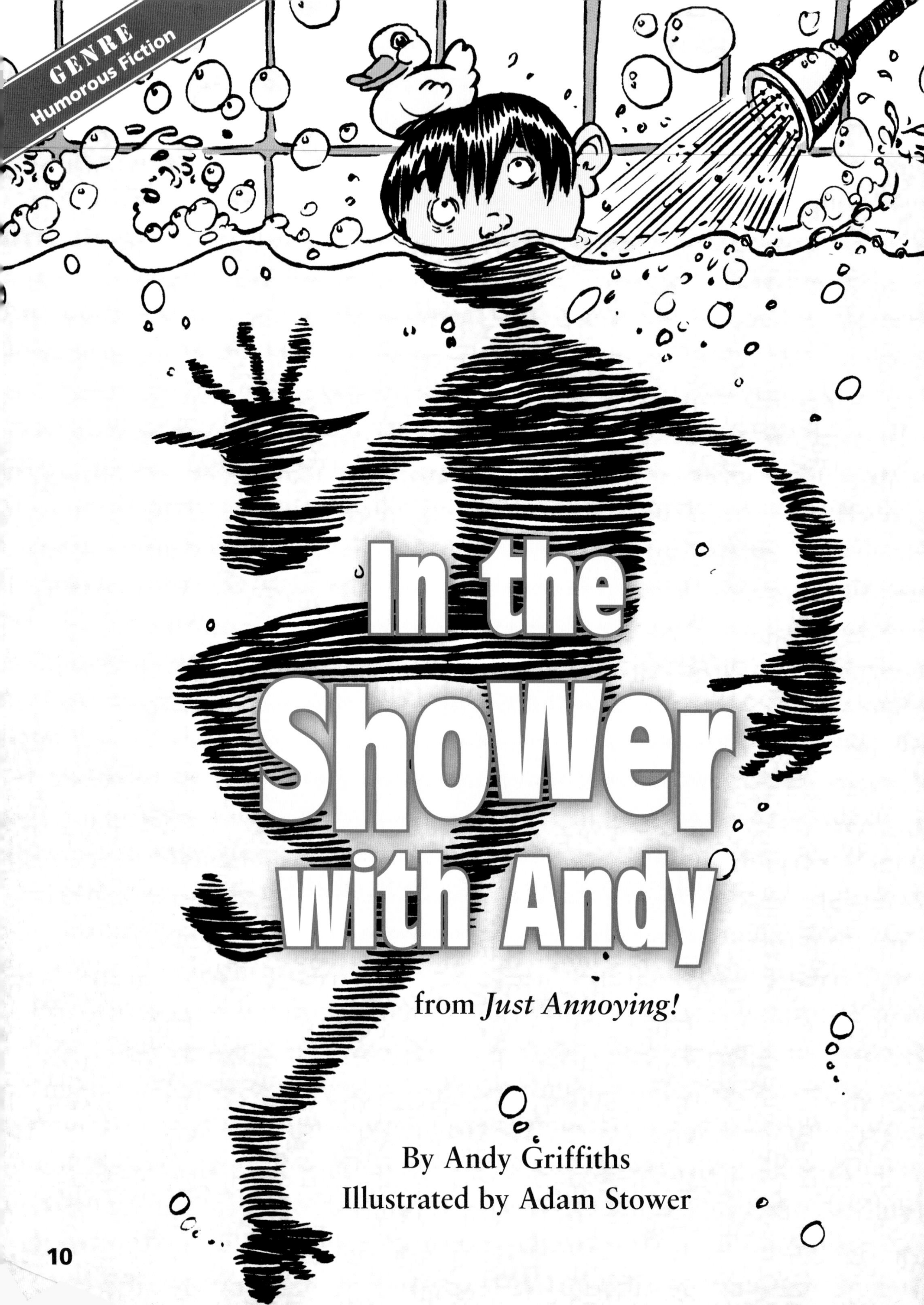

In the Shower with Andy

from *Just Annoying!*

By Andy Griffiths
Illustrated by Adam Stower

I'm in the shower. Singing. And not just because the echo makes my voice sound so cool either. I'm singing because I'm so happy.

Ever since I've been old enough to take showers, I've been trying to find a way to fill a shower **cubicle** up with water. If I put a washcloth over the drain I can get the water as far up as my ankles, but it always ends up leaking out through the gaps in the door.

But I think I've finally found the answer—Dad's caulk gun.

I've plugged up the drain.

I've sealed up the shower doors.

I've filled in all the cracks in the tiles.

The cubicle is completely watertight and the water is already up to my knees.

And the best thing is that I've got all night to enjoy it.

Mom and Dad have Mr. and Mrs. Bainbridge over for dinner. They'll be too busy listening to Mr. Bainbridge talking about himself to have time to worry about what I'm doing.

I hear banging on the door.

"Have you almost finished, Andy?"

It's Jen!

"No," I say. "I think I'm going to be in here a while yet."

"Can you hurry up?" yells Jen.

"But you already had your shower this morning," I yell.

"I'm going out," she says. "I need the bathroom!"

Bringing the Story to Life

The narration of the story sounds like Andy is talking directly to us. As you read, use a conversational tone of voice. Where applicable, act out parts of the story. For instance, you may bang on a wall or on the floor to simulate Jen's banging on the bathroom door. As the story becomes more suspenseful, gradually increase the urgency in your voice.

How deep do you think the water will get?

"Okay. I'll be out in a minute," I call. I always say that. It's the truth. Sort of. I will be out in a minute—I'm just not saying which minute it will be.

The cubicle is filling with thick white steam. Just the way I like it. Dad's always telling us how important it is to turn the fan on when we're taking a shower, but I don't see the point. A shower without steam doesn't make sense. You might as well go stand outside in the rain.

Jen bangs on the door again.

"Andy! Pleeeeease!"

"Okay," I call. "I'll be out in a minute."

"You said that a minute ago."

"I'm washing my hair."

"But you've been in there for at least half an hour. You don't have *that* much hair."

"I'm using a new sort of shampoo—I have to do it strand by strand."

"Andy!"

The water is almost up to my belly button.

There's only one thing missing. Bubbles!

I pick up the bubblebath and measure out a capful. I tip it into the water. A few bubbles, but not enough. I add another cap. And another. And another. One more for good measure. Another for good luck.

Do you think Andy should be adding so much bubble bath?

I keep adding bubblebath until the bottle is empty. The bubbles rise over my head. Cool. It's like I'm being eaten by this enormous white fungus. Well, not that being eaten by an enormous white fungus would be cool—it would probably be quite uncool, actually—but you know what I mean.

Jen is yelling. "Andy, if you don't get out right this minute, you're going to be sorry."

Jen is persistent, I'll give her that. But I'll fix her. I'll use my old "what did you say?" routine.

"Pardon?" I yell. "What did you say?"

"I said you're going to be sorry."

"What? I can't hear you!"

"I said get out of the shower!"

"Pardon?"

No reply. I win.

Aaaaagghhh!

The water's gone hot! Boiling hot!

Jen must have flushed the toilet. That's bad news.

I lose.

I jump back against the shower wall.

Hot water splatters onto my face. My chest. My arms.

I grab the cold tap and turn it on full.

The hot water disappears. Now it's freezing.

I'm going to have to turn both taps off and start all over again. I hate that. Being a pioneer is not easy.

I turn the hot tap off. But the cold won't budge.

I grab the tap with both hands. I try to twist it clockwise but it's stuck. Not even my superstrength can move it.

The caulk gun is hanging off the shower pipe. I pick it up and start bashing the tap with it. That should loosen it.

But the handgrip shatters.

The pieces disappear into the soapy water. I'm staring at a thin metal rod coming out of the wall. And the water is still flowing full blast.

Uh-oh! How is Andy going to stop the water?

I kneel down and clamp my teeth over the tap rod.

No good. The tap feels like it's rusted into place. My teeth will crack before it moves.

There's no steam left. The bubbles have been flattened. The freezing water is almost up to my chest. Maybe this wasn't such a great idea.

Time to **bail** out.

I take a deep breath and dive to the bottom of the shower. I'm trying to find the drain. I've got to get the caulk out before the shower fills up completely.

But I can't do it. I did the job too well. There's nothing but a hard, rubbery slab of caulk where the drain used to be. I can't poke through it. I can't get a fingernail underneath to lift it up. It's times like this I wish I didn't bite my nails. But then it's times like this that cause me to bite my nails in the first place.

Do you think this sort of thing happens to Andy often?

I stand up, gasping for air. The water is up to my neck. I grab hold of the door handle and try to wrench it open but I laid the caulk even thicker on the doors than the drain. If you ever want anything sealed tight I can recommend Dad's caulk gun. This stuff stays stuck forever.

I'm going to have to break the door down.

I'll use the gun. It made short work of the tap, so the door shouldn't be a problem.

I bash the glass with the gun handle. It bounces off. I bash it again, harder this time. The gun snaps in two. Just my luck. **Reinforced** shower door glass. Unbreakable.

I'm shivering. And not just from the cold. I'm scared.

I start bashing the door with the duck.

"HELP! I'M DROWNING! HELP!"

"I'm not surprised!" Jen yells back. "You've been in there long enough."

"Jen, I'm not kidding. Help me!"

"What did you say?" she says. "I can't hear you."

"Be serious," I yell. "I've caulked myself in here."

"What?"

She wins again.

Why won't Jen help Andy?

I'm treading water. My head is very close to the top of the shower.

The only way I can save myself is to get rid of the water.

I'm going to have to drink it.

Dirty, soapy shower water.

I'd rather die.

The water nudges the tip of my nose.

Actually, on second thought, I'd rather drink the water.

I start swallowing.

It's working. I just have to drink as fast as the shower is filling up. And if I can drink even faster, then I might get out of here alive yet. Actually the water doesn't taste that bad—it's only been three days since my last shower.

Yuck! Would you drink the shower water if you were Andy?

My head is bumping against the roof of the shower.

It's getting harder to breathe.

There's more banging on the door but it sounds like it's coming from a long way away.

"I'm going to tell Dad," says Jen in a distant voice. "Is that what you want? Is it?"

"Yes, Jen," I call. "Yes! Please hurry!"

Everything becomes quiet.

My life is flashing before my eyes.

I see myself blowing a high-pitched whistle while Mom is trying to talk on the telephone. I see myself letting air out of the tires on Dad's car. I see myself hiding a rubber snake in Jen's bed. Is that all I did with my life? Annoy people? Surely I did something useful . . . Something good?

Nope. I can't think of anything. Except for solving the problem of how to fill a shower cubicle with water.

I may be going to die, but at least it will be a hero's death. Future generations of Australian children will thank me as they float around in their sealed-up shower cubicles.

Do you think Andy will find a way to escape?

Ouch!

Something is pressing into the top of my head.

I look up.

The fan! I forgot all about it.

It's not very big, but it's better than nothing. If I can get the grille off, then I can escape through the hole and up into the roof.

I work my fingers under the edge of the grille and pull on it. It comes off easily.

I reach into the casing and grab hold of the fan. I rock it back and forth. There is a little bit of give in it. I start giving it all I've got.

Finally the bolts holding it give way. I push my arms and head into the hole, kicking like mad to get the boost I need to make it all the way up.

The opening is smaller than I thought. I **expel** every last bit of air in my lungs to make myself thin enough to fit through the hole. Not that there was much air left in them, but it seems to help.

At last! I'm through!

I'm lying on a yellow insulation patch above the ceiling of our house. The glass fibers are prickly on my skin, but I'm not complaining. It's a lot better than where I was. I reach down and pick up my rubber duck. We're in this together. I can't just leave it.

After I get my breath back, I look around.

I know there's a manhole in the top of the kitchen. All I have to do is to locate it, climb down into the kitchen and sneak down the hallway into my room. Then I can put my pajamas on and go to bed early. It will save a lot of boring explanations—and, if I'm really lucky, Jen will get the blame.

Do you think Andy's plan will succeed?

I have to move fast. I start crawling toward the kitchen. I'm carrying the duck in one hand and using my other hand to feel my way along the roof beam.

Suddenly I feel a sharp pain in my thumb.

I look at my thumb. A huge splinter is sticking out of it. I pull it out with my teeth. Ouch!

I shake my hand a few times and look around for my duck. It has landed in the middle of a large unsupported section of insulation. I'm tempted to leave it there. But that wouldn't be right. It's been with me all the way. I can't **abandon** it now.

I reach toward it but it's too far away. I'm going to have to crawl out there. I know you're not supposed to climb on the unsupported parts of the ceiling, but I think it will be okay. I'm not that heavy. And it's not as if I have any clothes on to weigh me down.

Uh-oh. This sounds dangerous! Should Andy go after his duck?

I climb carefully onto the unsupported section and start moving slowly to the center. One more foot and I'm there.

I pick up my duck and bring it up to my face. "Just you and me," I say.

The duck creaks. That's weird. I didn't know rubber ducks could talk.

Uh-oh. The creaking is not coming from the duck. It's coming from underneath me. The ceiling is giving way.

I try to grab the wooden beam but I can't reach it.

The ceiling caves in.

Next thing I know, I'm lying, legs spread, in the middle of the dinner table—my fall broken by an insulation mat.

As the dust from the ceiling plaster settles, I see Mr. and Mrs. Bainbridge and Mom and Dad staring down at me.

Jen is standing next to Dad, her bath towel draped over her shoulder. Her back is turned toward me, and she's so busy complaining to Dad that she doesn't seem to notice what has happened.

". . . I've asked him a million times but he just won't get out . . ." she's saying.

"Oh, dear," says Mom.

"Oh, my," says Mrs. Bainbridge.

For once in his life, Mr. Bainbridge is speechless.

"Oh, no," says Dad, shaking his head at me. "No, no, no!"

"Oh, yes," says Jen. "And I'll tell you what else . . ."

Dad nods in my direction.

Jen stops, turns around, and stares.

I cover myself with the rubber duck, swing my legs over the edge of the table, and stand up.

"I beg your pardon," I say. "I was looking for the kitchen."

Nobody says anything. They are all just staring at me, their faces and clothes white from the plaster dust.

I head toward the door as fast as I can.

As I'm about to exit, I turn toward Jen. She is still standing there, eyes wide.

"Well, what are you waiting for?" I say. "Shower's free!"

Talking About the Story

Have students discuss Andy's plan and explain why they think Andy's plan was a good one or not.

Invite students to talk about a time when they had a plan and it did not turn out as they had hoped.

Vocabulary in Action

Words From the Story

cubicle

In the story, Andy seals up the drain, door, and cracks in a shower cubicle. A cubicle is a small, enclosed space that is used for a particular activity.

- Ask which of these is probably a cubicle, a gymnasium or an office space. Why do you think so?
- Have students find places in the classroom that could serve as cubicles.

bail

Andy decides it's time to bail out after the water faucet breaks. If you bail out of a situation, you get out of it because it is getting difficult or dangerous.

- Ask which is an example of bailing, running away from a nest of angry wasps or watching an enjoyable movie. Why?
- Have students tell about a time that they had to bail out of a bad situation.

reinforce

Andy can't break the shower door because it is made of reinforced glass. If you reinforce something, you add something else to it to make it stronger or harder.

- Ask what vehicle would be reinforced, your mother's car or a truck that is protected by an extra layer of tough metal. Explain why.
- Have students glue two pieces of paper together to make reinforced paper.

expel

Andy expels the air from his lungs to make himself smaller. To expel something means to force it out.

- Ask which is being expelled, a man walking out a door or a fly being shooed out a window. Explain your answer.
- Have students pretend to expel something with their hands.

abandon

In the story, Andy says he can't abandon his rubber duck. Abandoning something means leaving it behind when you don't want to or should not.

- Ask students what has been abandoned, some clothes that someone tossed onto the side of the road days ago or a football on a roof that you are still trying to reach. Explain.
- Have students tell or make up a story about a time when they had to abandon something.

Vocabulary in Action

Words About the Story

impetuous

Andy seals up the shower without thinking about the trouble that might get him into. You could say that Andy is impetuous. Someone who is impetuous does things quickly, without thought or care.

- Ask students who is impetuous, someone who rushes into a dark cave without a flashlight or someone who tests the depth of a lake before going swimming. Explain your answer.
- Have students tell about a time when they or someone they know was impetuous.

dilemma

Andy knows he shouldn't try to go after his duck when he's above the ceiling, but he doesn't want to leave his duck behind. In other words, Andy has a dilemma. A dilemma is a situation without an easy solution, usually because all the choices are equally good or equally bad.

- Ask which is a dilemma, trying to choose which flavor of ice cream you want or trying to choose which of your best friends' parties to go to. Why?
- Have students use facial expressions and body language to express how it feels to have a dilemma.

resolutely

Once Andy realizes that he can't turn the water off, he is determined to find a way out of the shower cubicle. In other words, he acts resolutely. If you do something resolutely, you do it without changing your mind or giving up.

- Ask who is acting resolutely, someone who joins a school club and quits a few days later or someone who joins an athletic team and practices as hard as possible. Why do you think so?
- Have students tell about a time when they acted resolutely to get something done.

We Can Do Anything!

Have you ever doubted your ability to do something? These two poems tell different stories about courage and conquering doubt.

Vocabulary

Words From the Poems

These words appear in blue in the poems. Explain these words after the poems are read.

scoff **lament**
assail **steadfast**
optimistic

Words About the Poems

Explain these words after the poems are read, using context from the poems.

decisive **resigned**
gratifying

Getting Ready for the Read-Aloud

Show students the picture on page 23 and read the title aloud. Have them notice that these children are celebrating that they have overcome some great challenge. Explain that you're going to read two poems; the characters in both poems must make decisions about how they will react to challenges in their lives.

Discuss how every challenge comes with many choices and how you have to decide which solution works best for you. Explain that it takes courage to believe in yourself and not let others make you feel unable to achieve your goals.

The following phrases occur in the poems and can be briefly explained as you come to them: *buckled right in,* started working; *quiddit,* the desire to quit; *prophesy,* telling the future; *adieu,* goodbye; *scheme,* plan.

We Can Do Anything!

By Edgar A. Guest
Illustrated by Jennifer Emery

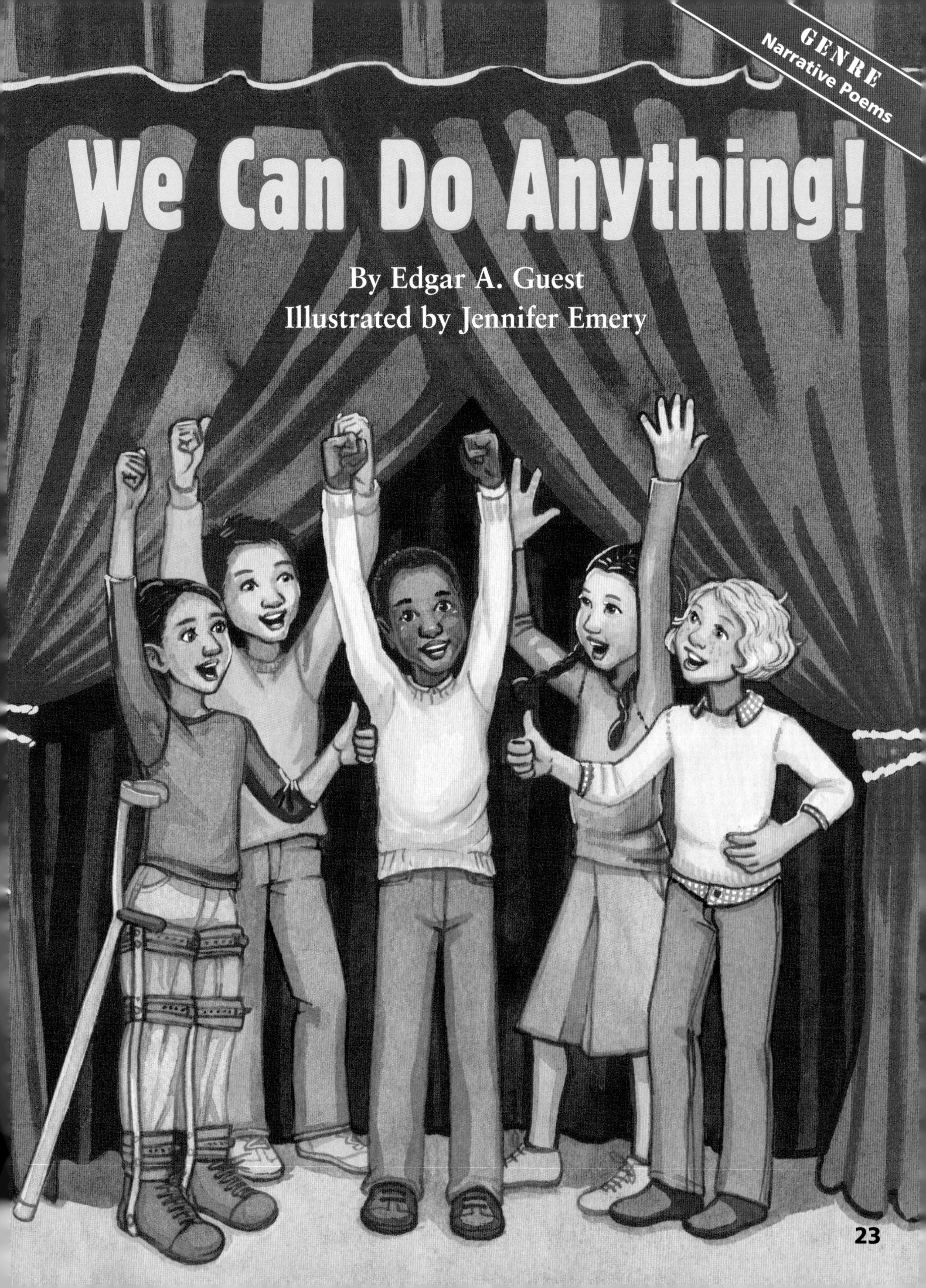

Bringing the Poems to Life

In both poems, read all the dialogue in an animated way. Display the facial and body expressions of someone who is determined or scoffing, pessimistic or optimistic as appropriate. Mimic physical elements of the poems, such as "took off his coat and took off his hat," "flung up his legs," and "swim around." The last lines of both poems should be infused with gusto!

Why did the character ignore the people who tried to change his mind?

"It Couldn't Be Done"

By Edgar A. Guest

Somebody said that it couldn't be done,
But he with a chuckle replied
That "maybe it couldn't," but he would be one
Who wouldn't say so till he'd tried.
So he buckled right in with the trace of a grin
On his face. If he worried he hid it.
He started to sing as he tackled the thing
That couldn't be done, and he did it.

Somebody **scoffed**: "Oh, you'll never do that;
At least no one ever has done it";
But he took off his coat and he took off his hat,
And the first thing we knew he'd begun it.
With a lift of his chin and a bit of a grin,
Without any doubting or quiddit,
He started to sing as he tackled the thing
That couldn't be done, and he did it.

There are thousands to tell you it cannot be done,
There are thousands to prophesy failure;
There are thousands to point out to you, one by one,
The dangers that wait to **assail** you.
But just buckle in with a bit of a grin,
Just take off your coat and go to it;
Just start to sing as you tackle the thing
That "cannot be done," and you'll do it.

Perseverance

Author Unknown

Two frogs fell into a deep cream bowl.
One was a wise, **optimistic** soul.
But the other took the gloomy view.
"We shall drown," he **lamented** with a sad adieu.
So with that final despairing cry,
He flung up his legs and said, "Goodbye."

What do you think just happened?

Said the other frog with a **steadfast** grin,
"I can't get out, but I won't give in!
I'll just swim around until my strength is spent,
Then when I die, I'll be more content."
Bravely he swam to work his scheme,
As his struggles began to churn the cream.
The more he kicked his legs a flutter,
The more the cream turned into butter.
On top of the butter, at last he stopped,
And out of the bowl he merrily hopped.
The moral you ask? Oh, it's easily found.
If you can't get out, keep swimming around.

Talking About the Poems

Have students tell what was similar about both poems (*e.g.*, theme) and what was different (*e.g.*, human characters vs. animal characters).

Ask students to describe what they would do if they were told something they wanted to do couldn't be done.

Vocabulary in Action

Words From the Poems

scoff

In the first poem, somebody scoffs, "Oh, you'll never do that." If you scoff at something, you talk about it in a way that shows you think it's silly.

- Ask who might make them scoff, a person in the desert building a boat, or a person on an island building a boat. Why?
- Have students say "sharks don't sleep" with a normal tone, then say it again with a scoffing tone.

assail

In the first poem, the author mentions "the dangers that wait to assail you." To assail something or someone is to attack them physically or verbally.

- Ask who is being assailed, the girl swimming in a calm lake or the girl attempting to swim in the ocean but who is pushed back to land by the waves?
- Have students mimic being assailed by a bee.

optimisitic

In the second poem, the first frog is described as an optimistic soul. If you are optimistic, you are hopeful and look at things in a positive way.

- Ask which person is optimistic, the person who goes out to play in the rain or the person who carries an umbrella on a sunny day. Explain your answer.
- Write a pessimistic statement on the board (e.g., Today is going to be horrible.) and ask students to change one word to turn it into an optimistic statement.

lament

In the second poem, the second frog laments his awful situation. If you lament something, you say how sad you are about it.

- Ask which is a lament, crying during a funeral or laughter at a wedding. Why?
- Ask students if they want to share anything they have lamented.

steadfast

The second frog has a steadfast grin despite being trapped in a cream bowl. If you are steadfast in doing something, you will not give up or be stopped from doing it.

- Ask which person is being steadfast about getting a cat, the boy who saves his allowance for six months or the boy who whines about wanting a cat whenever he remembers. Why is that?
- Have students say something that they are steadfast about.

Vocabulary in Action

Words About the Poems

decisive

The first frog needed to make a quick choice whether to work to save his life or give up. Another way to say the frog made a quick choice and then stuck to it is to say that the frog was decisive. If you are decisive, you make decisions quickly without changing your mind later.

- Ask students which is being decisive, being unable to pick paint colors for your room or raising your hand high in class when you know the answer to a question. Why do you think so?
- Have students tell about a time when they were decisive about something.

gratifying

In the first poem, the character was pleased that he could do something when others said he could not do it. In other words, he was gratified. Something gratifying makes you feel happy and proud of what you've done.

- Ask students which is gratifying, having someone compliment a painting they made or having someone insult a painting they made. Why?
- Have students share a story about something they did that was gratifying.

resigned

When the second frog thought he had no choice, he gave up. Another way to say that is to say he was resigned. If you are resigned to a bad situation, you accept it without complaining because you can't change it.

- Ask who is resigned, the runner who quits before crossing the finish line or the swimmer who tries to gain the lead. Explain.
- Have students describe a time when they were resigned on something before it was finished.

The Tour

The Tour is a true story about Lance Armstrong, a world-class athlete, and the day that turned out to be a turning point in the three-week-long Tour de France.

Vocabulary

Words From the Story

These words appear in blue in the story. Explain these words after the story is read.

eliminate **contender**
stationary **grimace**
incredulous

Words About the Story

Explain these words after the story is read, using context from the story.

fatigue **foil**
stamina

Getting Ready for the Read-Aloud

Show students the picture of Lance Armstrong on page 29 and read the title aloud. Explain that Armstrong has won the world's most difficult bike race seven times in a row—more often than any other person. Have them notice the yellow jersey he is wearing, which tells other riders of his position as leader in the race.

Explain that this is a true story of one man's courage and determination as he tries to win a grueling bike race, the Tour de France. Use a map to show students the European countries and cities that are mentioned in the story. Discuss the length of a kilometer (1.6 miles), and the rough terrain—both up and down mountains—riders must cover to win.

The following phrases can be briefly explained as you come to them: *full-out,* doing everything possible; *drive a big gear into the teeth of that wind,* riding fast and hard into a wind; *without an ounce of give-up,* without even thinking about quitting; *the fastest splits,* shortest time between checkpoints; *jack-hammered,* pounded hard and fast; *lactic acid,* the reason why you can feel your muscles burn if you run for a long time.

The Tour

from *It's Not About the Bike: My Journey Back to Life*

By Lance Armstrong

Bringing the Story to Life

Start by reading the first half of the story in a normal rhythm. As the story progresses, increase the cadence of the reading to emulate the speed that the bicyclists are traveling. Use physical gestures to accentuate words that have "visual" power, such as *crashed, jack-hammered, heart pounding,* and *grimace of pain.* Emphasize the last exciting moments of the race then slow down and read the final bit slowly. The race is over.

The Tour de France is the world's premier bike race known for its punishing intensity. During The Tour, various stages and time trials occur, some over relatively flat terrain, others through mountains. The rider with the lowest total time is awarded a yellow jersey to wear during the next stage of the race. On July 11, 1999, 27-year-old Lance Armstrong begins Stage 8 of The Tour, with the help of team director Johan's constant radio communication in his ear. Lance rides with one goal in mind: capture the yellow jersey.

It is called the Race of Truth. The early stages separate the strong riders from the weak. Now the weak would be **eliminated** altogether.

We arrived in Metz for the time trial, and in this one, unlike the brief Prologue, riders would have an opportunity to win or lose big chunks of time. It was 56 kilometers long, which meant riding full-out for more than an hour, and those riders who didn't make the time cut were gone, out of the race. Hence the phrase "Race of Truth.". . .

Early in the morning of the stage, I went out and previewed the course, but I was already familiar with it, because we had scouted it during training camp. It had two very big climbs, one 1.5K long and the other 4K long. The early part would be windy, then came the hills, and the final flats would be into a strong headwind. It was a course that favored strength, a rider who could drive a big gear into the teeth of that wind. It wasn't enough to be fast; I would have to be fast for over an hour.

Why did Lance take a look at the course before the race?

As I warmed up on a **stationary** bike, results filtered in. The riders went out in staggered fashion, two minutes apart, and Alex Zulle, the Swiss favorite who had suffered the unfortunate crash on the Passage du Gois, was the early leader with a time of a little over an hour and nine minutes. I wasn't surprised; Zulle was a strapping blond strongman without an ounce of give-up, as I would continue to learn throughout the race.

The pre-race favorite, Abraham Olano, set off on the course just in front of me. But as I waited in the start area, word came through that Olano had crashed on a small curve, losing about 30 seconds. He got back on his bike, but his rhythm was gone.

My turn. I went out hard—maybe too hard. In my ear, Johan kept up his usual stream of steady advice and information. At the first two checkpoints, he reported, I had the fastest splits.

Third checkpoint: I was ahead of Zulle by a minute and forty seconds.

Ahead of me, I saw Olano.

Olano had never been caught in a time trial, and now he began glancing over his shoulder. I jackhammered at my pedals.

I was on top of him. The look on Olano's face was **incredulous**, and dismayed. I caught him—and passed him. He disappeared behind my back wheel.

Johan talked into my ear. My cadence was up at 100 rpms. "That's high," Johan warned. I was pedaling too hard. I eased off.

Who do you think Johan is? How do you think he helps Lance?

I swept into a broad downhill turn, with hay bales packed by the side of the road. Now I saw another figure ahead of me. A rider was lying by the side of the road, injured and waiting for medical attention. I recognized the colors of the Cofidis team.

Bobby Julich.

He had lost control and skidded out on the turn. I would learn later that he had badly bruised his chest and ribs. His race was over.

I went into a tuck around the turn.

From out of the crowd, a child ran into the road.

I swerved wide to avoid him, my heart pounding.

Quickly, I regained my composure and never broke rhythm. Ahead of me, I saw yet another rider. I squinted, trying to make out who it was, and saw a flash of green. It was the jersey of Tom Steels of Belgium, a superb sprinter who'd won two of the flat early stages, and who was a **contender** for the overall title.

But Steels had started six minutes in front of me. Had I ridden that fast?

Johan, normally so controlled and impassive, checked the time. He began screaming into the radio.

"You're blowing up the Tour de France!" he howled. "You're blowing up the Tour de France!"

I passed Steels.

I could feel the lactic acid seeping through my legs. My face was one big **grimace** of pain. I had gone out too hard—and now I was paying. I entered the last stretch, into that headwind, and I felt as though I could barely move. With each rotation of my wheels, I gave time back to Zulle. The seconds ticked by as I labored toward the finish.

Finally, I crossed the line.

I checked the clock: 1:08:36. I was the winner. I had beaten Zulle by 58 seconds.

I fell off the bike, so tired I was cross-eyed. As tired as I have ever been. But I led the Tour de France again. As I pulled the yellow jersey over my head, and once more felt the smooth fabric slide over my back, I decided that's where it needed to stay.

Lance Armstrong first won the grueling Tour de France in 1999. After being diagnosed with cancer in 1996, winning the Tour just three years later was one of the most amazing comeback stories in sports history. By winning the over 2000-mile, three-week bike race, Lance defeated cancer, inspired millions, and championed the greatest test of human stamina in sports today. He went on to win the Tour the following six years.

Talking About the Story

Have students summarize what happened during the race and what surprised them the most in the story. Did they expect the story to end the way it did? Explain.

Ask students to describe what they like or do not like about racing others.

Vocabulary in Action

Words From the Story

eliminate

In the story, the weaker riders were eliminated from the race in the early stages. If you eliminate something, you remove it completely.

- Ask whose name has been eliminated from a list, the girl's name that was crossed off or the girl's name that was circled. Why?
- Have students tell which of their toys they have eliminated as they get older.

stationary

Lance Armstrong rides a stationary bike to warm up. Something that is stationary is not moving.

- Ask students which is more likely to be stationary, a puppy in the yard or their dinner on a plate. Explain your answer.
- Have students freeze in position and remain stationary for a count of five.

incredulous

Another rider in the story looks incredulous when Lance Armstrong passes him. If you are incredulous, you can't believe something because it is very surprising.

- Ask students which would make them incredulous, being told they had to go to school or seeing a pig fly overhead. Why?
- Have students try to look incredulous.

contender

Tom Steels was a contender for the overall title of the Tour de France. A contender is someone who competes to win a contest or an election, usually with a good chance of winning.

- Ask who might be a contender in the Olympics, a swimmer who trains every day, or a person who watches a lot of football on TV. Why do you think so?
- Have students tell about what they might be a contender for one day.

grimace

Toward the end of the race, Lance grimaces in pain. When you grimace, you twist your face in an ugly way because you are in pain or don't like something.

- Ask students when they might grimace, when they eat a sour lemon or when they eat a sweet piece of pie. Why do you think so?
- Have students grimace.

Vocabulary in Action

Words About the Story

fatigue

Lance becomes overly tired as he continues to ride. Another way to say that is to say fatigued. If you feel fatigue, you feel very, very tired.

- Ask students who might be fatigued, the person who worked hard all day or the person who went to a movie. Explain why.
- Have students try to look fatigued.

stamina

Lance has the strength and energy to stay in the race a long time. Another way to say that is to say he has stamina. Someone who has stamina can do something tiring for a long time.

- Ask students which they think takes more stamina, working long hours every day or working really hard for one hour. Why?
- Have students discuss some things that take stamina.

foil

Lance stops the other riders from winning the race. In other words he foils their attempts to win. If you foil someone's attempt to do something, you stop them from doing it.

- Ask students which child is foiling the attempt to have a nice family dinner, the one who sets the table or the one who refuses to sit and eat. Explain.
- Have students describe a time when they tried to do something but were foiled.

The Marble CHAMP

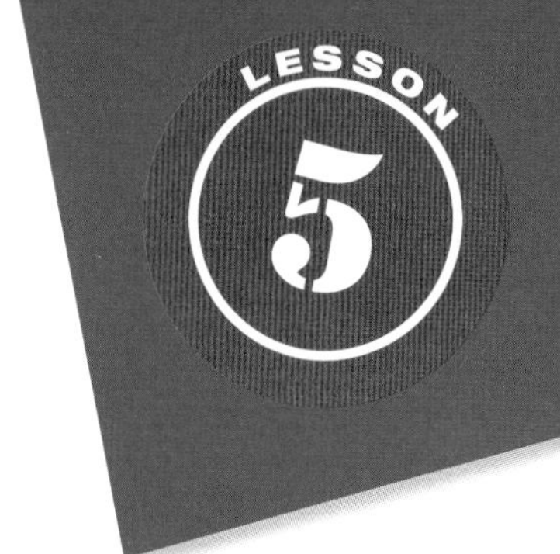

Lupe is terrible at every sport she tries. Finally, she finds a sport that she might actually be good at! However, Lupe still has to train and work hard to get the skills she needs to succeed.

Vocabulary

Words From the Story

These words appear in blue in the story. Explain these words after the story is read.

fume
opponent
rummage
glum
hypnotic

Words About the Story

Explain these words after the story is read, using context from the story.

dedication
victorious
seclusion

Getting Ready for the Read-Aloud

Show students the picture on pages 36–37 and read the title aloud. Explain that the girl is playing a game called marbles.

Ask students if any of them have ever played marbles. Then ask them to share what they know about the game. If necessary, explain some of its basic rules. Tell students that the game of marbles is played inside a ring drawn on the ground or floor. Players place all of their marbles inside the ring. Each player has a special marble called a shooter that they use to knock another player's marbles out of the ring. The person whose marbles are left inside the ring is the winner.

There are some phrases in the story that may be new to students. You might wish to briefly explain these phrases as you come to them: *milky agate,* a cloudy, white marble; *broke first,* shot the first marble.

GENRE
Realistic Fiction

The Marble CHAMP

from *Baseball in April and Other Stories*
By Gary Soto

Illustrated by Laurie Harden

Lupe Medrano, a shy girl who spoke in whispers, was the school's spelling bee champion, winner of the reading contest at the public library three summers in a row, blue ribbon awardee in the science fair, the top student at her piano recital, and the playground grand champion in chess. She was a straight-A student and—not counting kindergarten, when she had been stung by a wasp—never missed one day of elementary school. She had received a small trophy for this honor and had been congratulated by the mayor.

But though Lupe had a razor-sharp mind, she could not make her body, no matter how much she tried, run as fast as the other girls'. She begged her body to move faster, but could never beat anyone in the fifty-yard dash.

The truth was that Lupe was no good in sports. She could not catch a pop-up or figure out in which direction to kick the soccer ball. One time she kicked the ball at her own goal and scored a point for the other team. She was no good at baseball or basketball either, and even had a hard time making a hula hoop stay on her hips.

It wasn't until last year, when she was eleven years old, that she learned how to ride a bike. And even then she had to use training wheels. She could walk in the swimming pool but couldn't swim, and chanced roller skating only when her father held her hand.

Bringing the Story to Life

At the beginning of the story, Lupe is unsure of herself, so read this section in a more subdued way. As Lupe discovers her talent and becomes more confident, read with more animation and excitement in your voice. When you reach the part of the story that describes the championship, read the descriptions in a dramatic way to accentuate the suspense of the situation.

"I'll never be good at sports," she **fumed** one rainy day as she lay on her bed gazing at the shelf her father had made to hold her awards. "I wish I could win something, anything, even marbles."

At the word "marbles," she sat up. "That's it. Maybe I could be good at playing marbles." She hopped out of bed and **rummaged** through the closet until she found a can full of her brother's marbles. She poured the rich glass treasure on her bed and picked five of the most beautiful marbles.

She smoothed her bedspread and practiced shooting, softly at first so that her aim would be accurate. The marble rolled from her thumb and clicked against the targeted marble. But the target wouldn't budge. She tried again and again. Her aim became accurate, but the power from her thumb made the marble move only an inch or two. Then she realized that the bedspread was slowing the marbles. She also had to admit that her thumb was weaker than the neck of a newborn chick.

She looked out the window. The rain was letting up, but the ground was too muddy to play. She sat cross-legged on the bed, rolling her five marbles between her palms. Yes, she thought, I could play marbles, and marbles is a sport. At that moment she realized that she had only two weeks to practice. The playground championship, the same one her brother had entered the previous year, was coming up. She had a lot to do.

To strengthen her wrists, she decided to do twenty push-ups on her fingertips, five at a time. "One, two, three . . ." she groaned. By the end of the first set she was breathing hard, and her muscles burned from exhaustion. She did one more set and decided that was enough push-ups for the first day.

She squeezed a rubber eraser one hundred times, hoping it would strengthen her thumb. This seemed to work because the next day her thumb was sore. She could hardly hold a marble in her hand, let alone send it flying with power.

Why is Lupe's thumb sore?

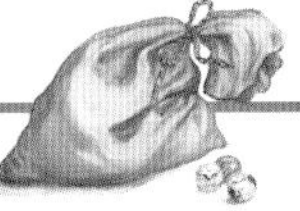

So Lupe rested that day and listened to her brother, who gave her tips on how to shoot: get low, aim with one eye, and place one knuckle on the ground.

"Think 'eye and thumb'—and let it rip!" he said.

After school the next day she left her homework in her backpack and practiced three hours straight, taking time only to eat a candy bar for energy. With a popsicle stick, she drew an odd-shaped circle and tossed in four marbles. She used her shooter, a milky agate with **hypnotic** swirls, to blast them. Her thumb *had* become stronger.

After practice, she squeezed the eraser for an hour. She ate dinner with her left hand to spare her shooting hand and said nothing to her parents about her dreams of athletic glory.

Practice, practice, practice. Squeeze, squeeze, squeeze. Lupe got better and beat her brother and Alfonso, a neighbor kid who was supposed to be a champ.

"Man, she's bad!" Alfonso said. "She can beat the other girls for sure. I think."

The weeks passed quickly. Lupe worked so hard that one day, while she was drying dishes, her mother asked why her thumb was swollen.

"It's muscle," Lupe explained. "I've been practicing for the marbles championship."

"You, honey?" Her mother knew Lupe was no good at sports.

"Yeah. I beat Alfonso, and he's pretty good."

That night, over dinner, Mrs. Medrano said, "Honey, you should see Lupe's thumb."

"Huh?" Mr. Medrano said, wiping his mouth and looking at his daughter.

"Show your father."

"Do I have to?" an embarrassed Lupe asked.

"Go on, show your father."

Reluctantly, Lupe raised her hand and flexed her thumb. You could see the muscle.

The father put down his fork and asked, "What happened?"

"Dad, I've been working out. I've been squeezing an eraser."

"Why?"

"I'm going to enter the marbles championship."

Her father looked at her mother and then back at his daughter. "When is it, honey?"

"This Saturday. Can you come?"

The father had been planning to play racquetball with a friend Saturday, but he said he would be there. He knew his daughter thought she was no good at sports and he wanted to encourage her. He even rigged some lights in the backyard so she could practice after dark. He squatted with one knee on the ground, entranced by the sight of his daughter easily beating her brother.

How does Lupe's dad feel about Lupe competing?

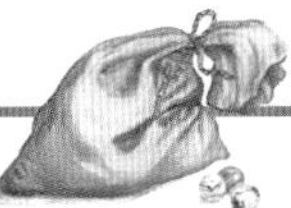

The day of the championship began with a cold blustery sky. The sun was a silvery light behind slate clouds.

"I hope it clears up," her father said, rubbing his hands together as he returned from getting the newspaper. They ate breakfast, paced nervously around the house waiting for 10:00 to arrive, and walked the two blocks to the playground (though Mr. Medrano wanted to drive so Lupe wouldn't get tired). She signed up and was assigned her first match on baseball diamond number three.

Lupe, walking between her brother and her father, shook from the cold, not nerves. She took off her mittens, and everyone stared at her thumb. Someone asked, "How can you play with a broken thumb?" Lupe smiled and said nothing.

She beat her first **opponent** easily, and felt sorry for the girl because she didn't have anyone to cheer for her. Except for her sack of marbles, she was all alone. Lupe invited the girl, whose name was Rachel, to stay with them. She smiled and said, "OK." The four of them walked to a card table in the middle of the outfield, where Lupe was assigned another opponent.

She also beat this girl, a fifth-grader named Yolanda, and asked her to join their group.

Why does Lupe invite Rachel and Yolanda to join her?

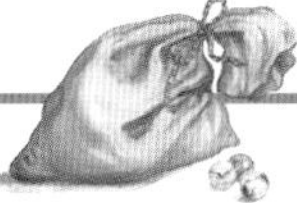

They proceeded to more matches and more wins, and soon there was a crowd of people following Lupe to the finals to play a girl in a baseball cap. This girl seemed dead serious. She never even looked at Lupe.

"I don't know, Dad, she looks tough."

Rachel hugged Lupe and said, "Go get her."

"You can do it," her father encouraged. "Just think of the marbles, not the girl, and let your thumb do the work."

The other girl broke first and earned one marble. She missed her next shot, and Lupe, one eye closed, her thumb quivering with energy, blasted two marbles out of the circle but missed her next shot. Her opponent earned two more before missing. She stamped her foot and said "Shoot!" The score was three to two in favor of Miss Baseball Cap.

The referee stopped the game. "Back up, please, give them room," he shouted. Onlookers had gathered too tightly around the players.

Lupe then earned three marbles and was set to get her fourth when a gust of wind blew dust in her eyes and she missed badly. Her opponent quickly scored two marbles, tying the game, and moved ahead six to five on a lucky shot. Then she missed, and Lupe, whose eyes felt scratchy when she blinked, relied on instinct and thumb muscle to score the tying point. It was now six to six, with only three marbles left. Lupe blew her nose and studied the angles. She dropped to one knee, steadied her hand, and shot so hard she cracked two marbles from the circle. She was the winner!

"I did it!" Lupe said under her breath. She rose from her knees, which hurt from bending all day, and hugged her father. He hugged her back and smiled.

Everyone clapped, except Miss Baseball Cap, who made a face and stared at the ground. Lupe told her she was a great player, and they shook hands.

How do you think Miss Baseball Cap feels?

A newspaper photographer took pictures of the two girls standing shoulder-to-shoulder, with Lupe holding the bigger trophy.

Lupe then played the winner of the boys' division, and after a poor start beat him eleven to four. She blasted the marbles, shattering one into sparkling slivers of glass. Her opponent looked on **glumly** as Lupe did what she did best—win!

The head referee and the President of the Fresno Marble Association stood with Lupe as she displayed her trophies for the newspaper photographer. Lupe shook hands with everyone, including a dog who had come over to see what the commotion was all about.

That night, the family went out for pizza and set the two trophies on the table for everyone in the restaurant to see. People came up to congratulate Lupe, and she felt a little embarrassed, but her father said the trophies belonged there.

Back home, in the privacy of her bedroom, she placed the trophies on her shelf and was happy. She had always earned honors because of her brains, but winning in sports was a new experience. She thanked her tired thumb. "You did it, thumb. You made me champion." As its reward, Lupe went to the bathroom, filled the bathroom sink with warm water, and let her thumb swim and splash as it pleased. Then she climbed into bed and drifted into a hard-won sleep.

Talking About the Story

Have students tell why Lupe was able to win the championship. Was she just lucky or did she earn her victory?

Ask students to say how they feel about Lupe. Did they want her to win? Why?

Vocabulary in Action

Words From the Story

fume

In the story, Lupe fumes because she is no good at sports. If you fume about something, you talk or think about it in an angry way.

- Ask who is fuming, someone who is thanking their parents for an amazing toy they received on their birthday or someone who is complaining about only receiving socks on their birthday. Why?
- Have students describe a situation that might have them fuming.

rummage

In the story, Lupe rummages through the closet and finds a can full of her brother's marbles. Rummaging through something means searching for something you want by moving things around in a hurried way.

- Ask whether someone might rummage through the kitchen cabinet looking for a snack or if someone would rummage through the sky looking for a star. Explain your answer.
- Have students name some places they have rummaged through to find things.

hypnotic

In the story, Lupe has a shooter marble with hypnotic swirls. Something that is hypnotic holds your attention so much that you can't think of anything else.

- Ask students which thing is hypnotic, a blaring car horn that makes you cover your ears or a swaying feather that you cannot take your eyes off of. Explain why.
- Have students follow your hypnotic fingers with their eyes.

opponent

In the story, Lupe plays against several opponents. An opponent is someone who is against you in a game, contest, or election.

- Ask students who their opponent would be in a football game, someone who tries to knock the ball out of their hands or someone who tries to pass them the ball so they can score. Explain.
- Have students describe a game or contest they were in and who their opponent was.

glum

The boy that Lupe beats looks glum. If you are glum, you are sad and quiet because you are unhappy about something.

- Ask students what might make them feel glum, having fun on the first day of summer vacation or being made fun of on the first day of school. Why do you think so?
- Have students show what a glum expression looks like.

Vocabulary in Action

Words About the Story

dedication

Lupe spends a lot of time practicing hard to become good at playing marbles. Another way to say that is that she is very dedicated. If you show dedication to something, you give it a lot of time and effort because you care so much about it.

- Ask who is showing their dedication to something, someone who spends days teaching their dog to sit or someone who does almost nothing but sit around. Why?
- Have students talk about something they did that took a lot of dedication. Why was it important for them to work so hard?

seclusion

Lupe spends a lot of time by herself practicing, and her family does not see her for a while. In other words, she goes into seclusion. If you are in seclusion, you are in a quiet place away from other people.

- Ask students who might be in seclusion, someone who takes time away from their noisy family to study for a hard test or someone who spends the day on a motorboat with friends. Explain your answer.
- Have students talk about a time they were in seclusion. What was good and what was bad about that time?

victorious

Lupe wins the playground marbles championship. Another way to say that is that she is victorious. You are victorious if you win a contest, sport, or battle.

- Ask students who is victorious, a person who comes in last place or a person who earns a "1st Place" trophy. Why do you think so?
- Have students share something they would like to be victorious at.

We Were There, Too!

Sometimes it seems like history is only made by adults. However, children have been involved in many important historical events, too. This passage describes two history-changing events that were all about young people.

Vocabulary

Words From the Stories

These words appear in blue in the stories. Explain these words after the stories are read.

lodge **tactic**

feverish **disband**

Words About the Stories

Explain these words after the stories are read, using context from the stories.

ingenuity **crucial**

anonymous **formative**

Getting Ready for the Read-Aloud

Show students the picture of the newsboys on page 46 and read the title aloud. Have them guess how old the newsies are. Explain that many years ago, children worked at jobs that today are done by adults. Explain that you'll be reading two stories about children working hard jobs.

Describe how life was difficult for these children, but they worked hard to earn money for themselves and their families.

Tell students that the situations told of in these stories can no longer take place. In 1938 the Fair Labor Standards Act was passed. This was the first U.S. child labor law making it illegal for children to be hired for certain kinds of work.

The following phrases occur in the story and can be briefly explained as you come to them: *fibers of lint,* tiny bits of dust from the cotton; *spindles and bobbins,* sticks that held the cotton as it was made into cloth; *textile mills,* factories that made cloth; *gouge,* to harm by taking something away from; *union,* an organization of workers that tries to improve working conditions.

GENRE
Historical Nonfiction

We Were There, Too!

By Phillip Hoose

Behind every major event in U.S history, there were young people who helped shape our nation. Whether by serving in wars, working in factories, or battling injustices, children have never been too young to make a difference.

Bringing the Stories to Life

These stories are fairly dramatic but they are still true. Be careful not to give them too melodramatic a reading. Encourage students to picture themselves in the story as you read.

Smith Wilkinson: The Same Thing Over and Over

Pawtucket, Rhode Island, 1790

Early on a Monday morning in December 1790, four small boys ducked through the frame door of an old furniture factory in Pawtucket, Rhode Island, and stepped into a gloomy room full of strange-looking machinery. It was still dark and so cold that the factory owner, Mr. Slater, told them to wait while he crawled out onto the ice-covered Blackstone River and smashed the ice with a stone. When water began to run freely over a great wheel, the machines groaned slowly to life. Shouting to be heard over the grinding gears and pounding wooden frames, Slater told ten-year-old Smith Wilkinson what to do. First, he said, take up a handful of cotton and pull it apart with both hands. Then put it all into your right hand. Then feed the cotton into your machine by moving your hand back and forth over the frame that sorts the cotton. That's it. Just keep doing it.

Does Smith's work sound interesting?

And that's what Smith did, except for two short breaks, until 7:30 that night. A few days later three more boys and then two girls joined the crew. The oldest was twelve and the youngest seven. Those nine children were the first factory workers in American history.

Ten years later there were one hundred children in that room. The youngest were only four years old. There were so many machines that the sound of clashing gears made hearing nearly impossible. The air was stuffy and filled with floating fibers of lint that got in their eyes and **lodged** fast in their lungs. As foremen inspected their work, children spread cleaned cotton onto a machine to be combed, and then passed it on to other children who operated a machine that turned the cotton into loose balls. They in turn passed it to more children who operated a machine that spun the cotton into yarn, arraying it onto dozens of spindles. The littlest children removed full bobbins, attached empty ones, and picked up and knotted broken threads. Sometimes when they got tired and slowed down or quit, they were beaten.

Aren't you glad that there is a law making this illegal?

Now that water-driven machines could spin cotton into yarn, redbrick textile mills sprang up along swift-moving New England rivers. Suddenly there was a huge demand for cotton to feed the machines, and a second machine soon accelerated the cloth-making process even more. In 1793, a Yale College graduate named Eli Whitney invented a device that let a man and a horse clean the seeds from cotton fifty times faster than by hand. Later, when the cotton "gin" (short for engine) was hitched to a steam engine, it could go twenty times faster than that.

The cotton gin's speed created a huge need for people to pick, bale, clean, and load cotton into barges. Planters **feverishly** bought up property and turned the South into a money-making land of cotton.

Kid Blink and the Newsies: Bringing Down Goliaths

New York City, 1899

William Randolph Hearst and Joseph Pulitzer were two of the richest and most powerful men in America in 1899.

Each owned a giant newspaper in New York City, and both competed to grab readers with sensational headlines and extra editions. They depended on a large network of city children and teenagers to get papers to readers. When the two millionaires tried to gouge the "newsies" for a few pennies more, it was nearly their downfall.

Newsies hollered out the day's headlines from busy street corners and subway entrances, from positions outside the revolving doors of office buildings, and from sidewalks near the lunch counters where secretaries and businesspeople grabbed quick meals. Some newsies stayed on the streets all day long, avoiding school, while others raced to their positions as soon as school was finished. They made their profits by buying papers from the newspaper company and then selling them to readers for a little more, pocketing the difference. They kept about a nickel for every ten papers they sold. If they didn't sell a paper, they had to take the loss. It was a tough deal, but a straight deal: At least a newsie knew what to expect.

The trouble started when Hearst and Pulitzer decided to make up for slow sales by raising the price that newsies had to pay for their papers. They didn't figure boys could do anything about it. They were very wrong. In July of 1899, three hundred newsies gathered in City Hall Park and formed their own union. They elected officers and made up committees. They announced that they would refuse to deliver Hearst's *New York Journal* or Pulitzer's *New York World* until their buying price went back to normal. "We're here for our rights and we will die defendin' 'em," explained ten-year-old Boots McAleenan to reporters.

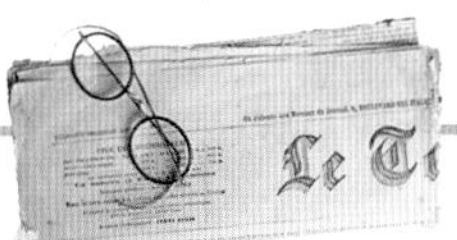

What were the newsies upset about?

The strike lasted two weeks. The newsies demonstrated at the places where delivery carts usually gave them their bundles of papers. They put signs up on nearby lampposts that read HELP THE NEWSBOYS and OUR CAUSE IS JUST. Their **tactics** were not gentle: Sometimes hundreds of boys surrounded the carts and threatened the drivers, who quickly tossed the papers over the side and fled. Mobs of boys threw rocks at the men Hearst and Pulitzer hired to replace them.

Soon nobody would even pick up the papers for fear of being confronted by angry boys. Police were caught in the middle—the public supported the newsies, but the companies and replacement workers demanded protection. And boys could almost always outrun the police.

Do you think it was right for the newsies to throw rocks?

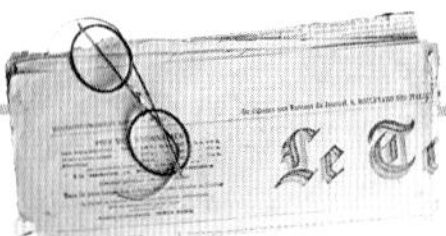

The newsboys' strike spread throughout New Jersey, Connecticut, and Massachusetts. As newspaper sales dropped, Pulitzer and Hearst began to lose big money. Advertisers demanded lower rates because of the strike. But other New York newspapers cheerfully made heroes of the newsies. Pulitzer's assistant sent him a worried message: "The people seem to be against us; they are encouraging the boys and tipping them . . . and refraining from buying the papers for fear of having them snatched from their hands."

One summer night the newsies organized a mass rally in lower Manhattan and five thousand boys showed up. A great cheer arose when a leader named Kid Blink vaulted up onto the speakers' platform. He raised his hands for silence and scratched his head as if something were puzzling him. "I'm trying to figure it out," he said, "how ten cents on a hundred papers can mean more to a millionaire than it does to newsboys, and I can't see it." The newsies vowed to continue the strike until they brought Pulitzer and Hearst to their knees.

When sales dropped by two-thirds, Hearst and Pulitzer gave up. They offered a deal that kept the prices the same but let the newsies return unsold papers and get their money back. In the end it meant more money than before. The newsies took it, **disbanded** their union, and went back to selling papers.

Talking About the Stories

Ask students to describe the kinds of work Smith Wilkinson, Kid Blink, or Boots McAleenan did.

Ask students to summarize the stories and describe how they felt as they heard about the children and their working conditions.

Vocabulary in Action

Words From the Stories

lodge

In the story of Smith Wilkinson, the fibers from the cotton lodged in the children's lungs. If an object lodges somewhere, it gets stuck there.

- Ask students which is lodged, a pebble jammed into the sole of their shoe or a pebble rolling around inside their shoe. Explain.
- Have students describe a time when something was lodged where it shouldn't have been and how they fixed the situation.

feverish

After the cotton gin was created, the planters feverishly bought property in the South to plant cotton. If you do something feverishly, you do it very quickly, as if you need to finish it as soon as possible.

- Ask who is writing feverishly, the boy who needs to write a full page in the last minute of a testing hour or the boy who needs to write a sentence sometime during a whole class period. Explain your answer.
- Have students describe something they did feverishly. Why were they in such a hurry?

tactic

The newsies used tough tactics to get what they wanted. A tactic is something you do to try to get what you want.

- Ask students what would be a good tactic for getting a larger allowance, doing more chores around the house or losing all their lunch money. Why do you think so?
- Have students describe a tactic they used to get something they wanted. Did the tactic work or not?

disband

Once the newsies got what they wanted, they disbanded their union. If a group disbands, it stops doing things together as a group.

- Ask which is disbanded, a music group that meets every week to play together or a music group where each member has decided to do something else with other people. Why?
- Have students talk about a group they know of that disbanded. Why did this happen?

Vocabulary in Action

Words About the Stories

ingenuity

The newsies solved their problem creatively. You could say they used ingenuity to get what they wanted. If you have ingenuity, you are good at finding new ways to solve problems and make things.

- Ask which takes more ingenuity, inventing a new toy or reading a newspaper. Why?
- Have students describe something they've done that took ingenuity. Why did they want to do it? How did they do it?

anonymous

We know the names of Smith Wilkinson and Kid Blink, but we don't know the names of most of the children who worked with them. You could say these children were anonymous. If you are anonymous, other people don't know your name or that you were the one who did something.

- Ask who is anonymous, the person who signs a letter as "a secret admirer" or the person who signs a letter with their name. Explain your answer.
- Ask students when they might want to be anonymous.

crucial

Winning the strike mattered more than almost anything else to the newsies. You could say it was crucial to them. If something is crucial, it is very important.

- Ask which is more crucial, getting a good grade on a test or playing a video game. Why?
- Have students describe something that is crucial to their happiness.

formative

Working shaped the lives of the children in factories and the newsies. You could say it was a formative experience for them. A formative experience is one that plays an important part in the kind of person you become.

- Ask students which is a formative experience, learning to read or learning to snap their fingers. Explain.
- Have students describe a formative experience in their lives.

MACAVITY: The Mystery Cat

This poem uses humor, exaggeration, mystery, and surprise to paint a picture of a wily character who can get away with anything.

Vocabulary

Words From the Poem

These words appear in blue in the poem. Explain these words after the poem is read.

levitate
astray
neglect
alibi
stifle

Words About the Poem

Explain these words after the poem is read, using context from the poem.

enigma
notorious
escapade

Getting Ready for the Read-Aloud

Show students the picture of Macavity on page 54 and read the title aloud. Explain that the cat is leaving the scene of a crime. Point out the detectives trying to find Macavity. Ask students if they think Macavity will get caught.

Explain that this poem is about a mysterious cat who commits a lot of crimes and never gets caught. Ask students if they have cats. Have students describe how cats act and move and ask them if they have ever seen a cat darting in and out of dark places.

The following terms or phrases occur in the poem and can be briefly explained as you come to them: *Scotland Yard,* police detectives in England; *fakir,* miracle worker; *Peke,* short for pekingese: a little yappy dog; *Foreign Office find a Treaty's gone astray,* the government discovers that important papers have been lost; *Napoleon of Crime,* a person who controls the world of crime.

GENRE
Narrative Poem

MACAVITY: The Mystery Cat

By T. S. Eliot

Illustrated by Edward Gorey

Macavity's a Mystery Cat: he's called the Hidden Paw—
For he's the master criminal who can defy the Law.
He's the bafflement of Scotland Yard, the Flying Squad's despair:
For when they reach the scene of crime—*Macavity's not there!*

Macavity, Macavity, there's no one like Macavity,
He's broken every human law, he breaks the law of gravity.
His powers of **levitation** would make a fakir stare,
And when you reach the scene of crime—*Macavity's not there!*
You may seek him in the basement, you may look up in the air—
But I tell you once and once again, *Macavity's not there!*

Macavity's a ginger cat, he's very tall and thin;
You would know him if you saw him, for his eyes are sunken in.
His brow is deeply lined with thought, his head is highly domed;
His coat is dusty from **neglect**, his whiskers are uncombed.
He sways his head from side to side, with movements like a snake;
And when you think he's half asleep, he's always wide awake.

Macavity, Macavity, there's no one like Macavity,
For he's a fiend in feline shape, a monster of depravity.
You may meet him in a by-street, you may see him in the square—
But when a crime's discovered, then *Macavity's not there!*

He's outwardly respectable. (They say he cheats at cards.)
And his footprints are not found in any file of Scotland Yard's.
And when the larder's looted, or the jewel-case is rifled,
Or when the milk is missing, or another Peke's been **stifled**,
Or the greenhouse glass is broken, and the trellis past repair—
Ay, there's the wonder of the thing! *Macavity's not there!*

Bringing the Poem to Life

Stress the rhythm and cadence. Fluctuate the tone as you repeatedly read the line "Macavity's not there!" from soft hush to loud declaration. Use an awestruck tone as you list the increasing seriousness of Macavity's crimes. As you read, demonstrate unfamiliar phrases—miming a private eye with a magnifying glass for "Scotland Yard" or striking an imperial stance for "Napoleon of Crime."

Does Macavity look like what you expect a master criminal to look like?

And when the Foreign Office find a Treaty's gone **astray**,
Or the Admiralty lose some plans and drawings by the way,
There may be a scrap of paper in the hall or on the stair—
But it's useless to investigate—*Macavity's not there!*
And when the loss has been disclosed, the Secret Service say:
"It *must* have been Macavity!"—but he's a mile away.
You'll be sure to find him resting, or a-licking of his thumbs,
Or engaged in doing complicated long division sums.

How do you think Macavity manages to always get away?

Macavity, Macavity, there's no one like Macavity,
There never was a Cat of such deceitfulness and suavity.
He always has an **alibi**, and one or two to spare:
At whatever time the deed took place—MACAVITY WASN'T THERE!
And they say that all the Cats whose wicked deeds
are widely known
(I might mention Mungojerrie, I might mention Griddlebone)
Are nothing more than agents for the Cat who all the time
Just controls their operations: the Napoleon of Crime!

Talking About the Poem

Have students tell what their favorite part of the poem was. Why did they choose that part?

Ask students if they know any cats that could be master criminals. Have them explain their reasons.

Vocabulary in Action

Words From the Poem

levitate

The poem refers to Macavity's powers of levitation. If someone or something levitates, they appear to rise and float in the air without anything to support them.

- Ask who might make something levitate, a stage magician or a school teacher. Explain your answer.
- Ask if students have ever seen something levitate, whether on a television show or in a movie.

neglect

In the poem, Macavity is said to neglect his appearance, which is why his fur is dusty and his whiskers are not combed. If you neglect something, you fail to take care of it properly.

- Ask students which has been neglected, a lawn full of weeds with grass up to their waists or a lawn that's trim and green with a border of flowers. Why do you think so?
- Have students talk about a time when they neglected something. Why did they do that?

stifle

In the poem, Macavity stifles a Peke, making the little yappy dog be quiet. If you stifle something that is happening, you force it to stop.

- Ask which is stifled, a radio playing music or an alarm clock covered with a pillow so no one can hear the beeping. Why?
- Have students pretend to stifle laughter.

astray

In the poem, an important government paper—a treaty—has gone astray. Something that has gone astray has gone missing while it is on its way somewhere.

- Ask students which has gone astray, a letter to them that arrives at their house or a letter to a stranger that arrives at their house. Why is that?
- Have students give examples of when they went astray.

alibi

In the poem, Macavity always has an alibi. If you have an alibi for something, you can prove that it was not your fault or you were somewhere else when it happened.

- Ask students when they would want an alibi, when a crime has been committed in their neighborhood or when a new neighbor has moved in. Explain.
- Ask students who would be able to give them an alibi for a crime that's happening right now.

Vocabulary in Action

Words About the Poem

enigma

In the poem, there is no explanation for how Macavity leaves the scene of his crimes. In other words, his escapes are enigmas. Something that is an enigma is mysterious and difficult to understand.

- Ask students which would most likely be an enigma, the reason the sky is blue or what time they have to go to bed. Explain why.
- Ask students if they can think of any other enigmas.

escapade

In the poem, Macavity takes a lot of exciting risks. You could also say that he goes on escapades. A daring adventure or action can be called an escapade.

- Ask which event seems more like an escapade, staying at home or going on a week-long camping trip. Why?
- Have students talk about an escapade they'd like to go on.

notorious

It is clear that Macavity is known for committing crimes and disappearing. You could also say that he is notorious for these actions. To be notorious means to be well-known for something bad.

- Ask whether someone is more likely to be notorious for robbing a bank or for writing a popular book. Explain.
- Have students name some people who are notorious. What are they notorious for?

Bigfoot Cinderrrrrrella

This twist on the traditional fairy tale of Cinderella tells of a nature-loving girl named Rrrrrella who wins a contest at the Bigfoot prince's annual fun-fest and becomes his bride.

Vocabulary

Words From the Story

These words appear in blue in the story. Explain these words after the story is read.

lurch **putrid**
primp **rowdy**

Words About the Story

Explain these words after the story is read, using context from the story.

jovial **allure**
outlandish **suave**

Getting Ready for the Read-Aloud

Show students the picture of Rrrrrella on page 60 and read the title aloud. Explain that Rrrrrella is strong and carrying logs that she has chopped down from a tree. Have them notice the expression on her face.

Explain that this story is similar to the fairy tale, "Cinderella." Ask students to share what they know about this story. If necessary, explain that Cinderella has two stepsisters who put her to work and do not let her go to the ball. Cinderella's fairy godmother sends her to the ball wearing a beautiful dress and glass slippers. When she mistakenly leaves one of her slippers behind, a handsome prince searches for the owner of the slipper and soon finds that it belongs to Cinderella.

There are some words in the story that may be new to students. You might wish to briefly explain these words as you come to them: *odoriferous,* giving off a smell; *coniferous,* having pine cones; *deadfalls,* fallen trees and tangled bushes; *clogs,* heavy, wooden shoes; *clan,* a large group of relatives.

GENRE
Fantasy

Bigfoot Cinderrrrrella

By Tony Johnston
Illustrated by
James Warhola

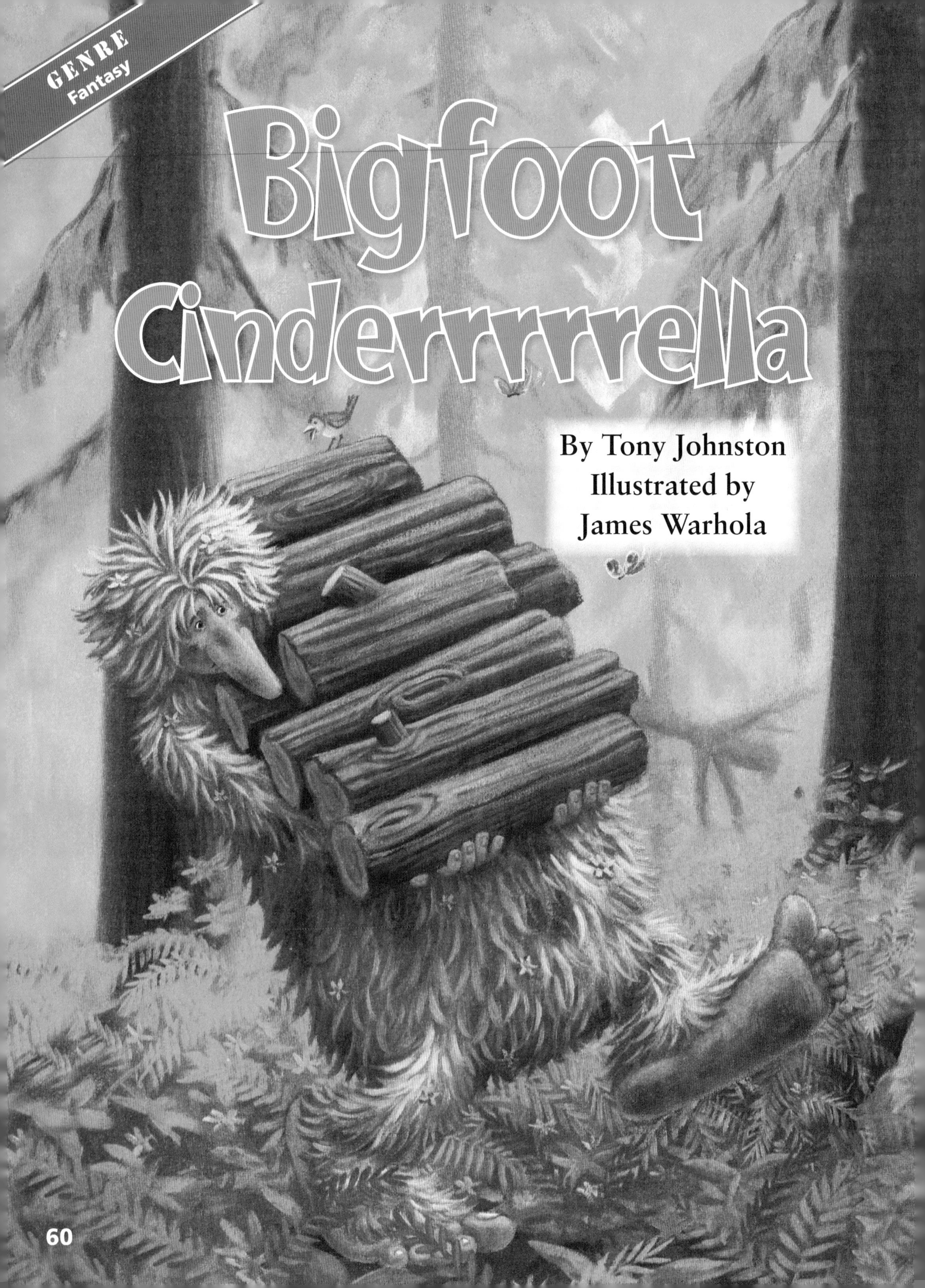

Once upon a time, in the old-growth forest, a band of Bigfoots lived. An enormous snag towered above the other trees close to their camp. Inside its hollow halls of bark lived a dashing Bigfoot prince.

He was tall and dark as a Douglas fir—with feet like cedar stumps. He was as odoriferous as his tree-home was coniferous. And so horrendously hairy that Bigfoot women near and far longed to marry him.

Bringing the Story to Life

Read the dialogue dramatically, using different voices for the Bigfoot prince, Bigfoot stepsisters, and Ella (Rrrrrella). Use sound effects for words such as "poof," "THUNK," and "floop." While you read, use your hands and face to demonstrate such phrases as "They teased her like singing mosquitos" and "when she shambled home empty-handed."

Whenever they saw him **lurching** along they blocked his path like deadfalls. They draped wildflowers around themselves. They batted their matted eyelashes, to stun him into love.

But the prince loved nature best.

"*No pick flowers!*" he bellowed at them in a voice as rough as bark.

Why do you think the Bigfoot prince got angry when he saw Bigfoot women picking flowers?

In this place there lived a Bigfoot woman and her three daughters. Well, really, only two were hers. The third was a stepchild.

The daughters were puny things with dinky feet, almost furless as Bigfoots go, and as sour as little green berries. They spent their days bathing and picking their teeth with fishbones and sleeking their fur with pinecones. For fun, they threw rocks at spotted owls.

The stepdaughter was just the opposite—nearly as woolly as a mammoth, golden as a banana slug, with feet like log canoes. She loved nature and would harm no creature.

Her stepsisters despised her and they made her work. Although her name was Ella, they roared at her so much that everyone called her Rrrrrella.

"*Rrrrrella, fix fire!*"

"*Rrrrrella, catch fish!*"

They forced her to comb her fur—and stick wildflowers in it! If she tugged them out, they put back twice as many!

Is Rrrrrella's life easy?

In spite of this **primping**, Rrrrrella was sooty from the fire and stinking with fish. So they teased her like stinging mosquitos.

"You beast." They laughed and held their noses.

"You positively rrrrreek."

"You absolute fffffreak!"

Then they bathed her a lot in the creek.

"EEEEEK!"

One morning, Rrrrrella went to the river to get supper. She fished all day, and tossed her catch onto the bank in a silvery pile.

Suddenly, a grizzly bear appeared. He seemed hungry. Rrrrrella was bigger than the bear, so she could have shooed him away. But she was too kind. She let him have the fish.

When she shambled home empty-handed, her stepsisters rubbed their bellies and bellowed, *"Food! Food! Food!"* They forced her to fish all night.

Now, every year the Bigfoot prince gave a great fun-fest. There were gifts and food, and games—like jump-the-fire, bear-cave hide-and-seek, and hurl the hemlock. But logrolling was the favorite. This year whichever woman rolled the prince off a log and into the river would become his wife.

Rrrrrella's puny sisters hoped to dunk the prince.

"When me snag **putrid** furball prince, me rule whole tree-place!" yelled the older one.

"Me pick all flowerrrrr!" The younger one grinned.

Then they bellowed together, "Powerrrrr! Powerrrrr! Powerrrrr!"

Do you think that Rrrrrella will be allowed to go to the fun-fest?

So they smoothed their pitiful fur. Then, spruced up with wildflowers and wearing fine bark-clogs to grip the log, they clomped to the festival.

"Me go too?" Rrrrrella hollered after them. She adored to sweat and win at games.

Her sisters hooted so hard, they fell down.

"You stay. Catch plenty fish. We catch prince."

How Rrrrrella longed to go! Sadly, she stared at the river. She saw a fish jump. She made a wish on the fish. "Me wish go fun-fest. Me wish dunk prince."

"Heartfelt wish is true wish," growled a gruff voice. "And so, you go."

Rrrrrella spun around. She was staring at a bear, the very one she had given fish.

"Who you?" she asked.

"Me your beary godfather."

Rrrrrella was overjoyed—then underjoyed.

She mumbled, "Me got no bark-clogs, to keep on log. Feets too big."

"No be bugbrain," snorted her godfather. He swiped the air with a paw, and, instantly, an enormous pair of clogs appeared.

Rrrrrella tried them on. They fit perfectly.

Then the grizzly waved a paw over her and—poof—the wildflowers she wore were dust. He patted and matted her fur, and it tangled like the very forest floor.

She boomed, "THANKS!" and gave him a crunching hug.

"Be back sundown!" he warned. "Or you be like sisters make you. No furry and smelly. But plenty flowery."

Rrrrrella wasn't worried. She had lots of time. She skipped off, shaking the whole forest as she went.

At the fun-fest, there were Bigfoot women from every clan. The games had begun. One by one the women leaped onto a log where the prince crouched, ready. One by one he dumped them into the water.

Rrrrrella's stepsisters hated games. But to catch the prince they'd do anything—even give logs a twirl. And they hoped a good drenching might even wash off his stench. But they never got the chance. When their turn came, the prince saw their wildflower-chains and glowered. He tossed them in the water, snarling, "*NO PICK FLOWERS!*"

The day grew late. Everyone had tried to win. Everyone had failed.

The Bigfoot prince rumbled, "*Rrrrrats! No brrrrride!*" He was about to slouch home when—THUNK!—Rrrrrella bounded onto the log, pounding her chest and whooping, "ME DUNK PRINCE!"

Grunting with all her might, she spun the log like a big twig. Then she gave it a twist and—*floop!*—the prince flopped into the river.

There was a stunned silence. The Bigfoots were slow-witted, so it took them a while to figure out what had happened. When at last they began to chant, "*Brrrrride! Brrrrride! Brrrrride!*" the sun was setting!

Should Rrrrrella be worried about this? Why?

Rrrrrella saw that and rushed into the dense trees, shrieking, "EEEEEK!" just as her matted fur went sleek and wildflowers began to sprout.

The prince lurched from the water, dripping and crushed. His dream woman—shaggy as the forest floor, smelly as a fish, and strong—was gone.

Scratching his craggy head, he slumped down on a boulder.

"*Drrrrrat! Drrrrrat! Drrrrrat!*" He gnashed his mossy teeth. "*Where my stinking beauty go?*"

Then he saw one big bark clog. Hers! Now perhaps he *could* find his princess.

The prince shuffled from snag to snag, cave to cave, lugging the lost clog. But though all the Bigfoot women tried it on, it was too large for anyone.

The moment he reached Rrrrrella's cave, her stepmother and stepsisters pounced on the prince, wrestled the clog from him, and jumped into it eagerly. Their feet were so small, they all fit at once!

Then Rrrrrella bounded up, yelling, "Me trrrrry! Me trrrrry! ME! ME! ME!"

She did. And her foot fit the clog like a seed in a pod.

When she pulled out its mate, the Bigfoot prince knew he'd found his bride. He thumped his chest and roared with joy.

The stepsisters roared too. In tantrums, they yanked up some wildflowers and saplings. Their mother kicked the prince black and blue.

Soon there was a **rowdy** wedding in the old-growth forest. Everyone was invited. Even Rrrrrella's stepmother and stepsisters could come—if they followed these rules carefully:

No pick flower.

No pull tree.

No kick royal family.

Talking About the Story

Have students tell their favorite part in the story and explain why they liked it.

Invite students to talk about a time when someone was kind enough to help them do something that they could not do on their own.

Vocabulary in Action

Words From the Story

lurch

In the story, the Bigfoot prince lurches through the forest. If you lurch, you make a sudden, jerky movement forward.

- Ask students what animal probably lurches, an ant crawling up a mound of dirt or angry gorillas bounding towards each other. Why do you think so?
- Have students practice lurching.

primp

After her stepsisters force her to primp, Rrrrrella is still dirty. If you primp, you take a long time getting ready because you are picky about how you look.

- Ask who is primping, someone trying get the part in their hair perfectly straight or someone taking a quick shower. Explain your answer.
- Have students name some people they know who enjoy primping.

putrid

One of Rrrrrella's stepsisters describes the Bigfoot prince as being putrid. Something that is putrid is rotten and smells awful.

- Ask which smells putrid, old garbage or cherry perfume. Explain why.
- Have students use facial expressions and body language to show how they would act if there was something putrid in the room.

rowdy

At the end of the story, there is a rowdy wedding. If people are rowdy, they are noisy and rough and may end up causing trouble.

- Ask where someone might be rowdy, at the library or at an exciting basketball game. Why?
- Have students tell about a time when they were rowdy.

Vocabulary in Action

Words About the Story

jovial

Rrrrrella is very happy when her beary godfather gives her bark-clogs to wear to the fun-fest. Another way to say that is that she is jovial. If someone is jovial, they are happy and behave in a cheerful way.

- Ask which would make you jovial, hanging out with your friends or hanging clothes in a closet. Explain your answer.
- Have students use facial expressions and body language to show how they act when they are jovial.

outlandish

It would be strange and unusual if many women actually wanted to marry a hairy, smelly prince. You could say that it would be outlandish. If something is outlandish, it is weird and unlikely to happen.

- Ask which might be considered outlandish, a leopard with spots or an elephant with spots. Explain why.
- Have students make up an outlandish story.

allure

Rrrrrella is a dream woman to the prince; she is shaggy, smelly, and strong. You could say that the prince cannot resist her allure. The allure of something is the way it is attractive or exciting.

- Ask students what has a stronger allure, the idea of flying to an amusement park or the idea of walking home. Why do you think so?
- Have students describe the allure of a place they would like to go.

suave

Unlike the Bigfoot prince, most princes in fairy tales are handsome and charming. In other words, they are suave. Someone who is suave is charming, polite, and elegant, but may not be sincere.

- Ask students who they would expect to be suave, a salesperson or a scientist. Why?
- Have students take turns acting and talking in a suave manner.

A President's Bumpy Ride

This piece tells the humorous story of how our nation's 8th president, Martin Van Buren, took a nasty spill on the National Road, the first road funded by the U.S. government.

Vocabulary

Words From the Story

These words appear in blue in the story. Explain these words after the story is read.

jolt **prospect**
pry **incident**

Words About the Story

Explain these words after the story is read, using context from the story.

dumbfounded **isolated**
vindicate **refurbish**

Getting Ready for the Read-Aloud

Show students the picture of the road on page 70 and read the title aloud. Explain that the angry man is our 8th president, Martin Van Buren. Have students notice the rough state of the road, the mudhole, and the large root sticking out into the road.

Explain that this is a true story that took place in the 1800s, before the existence of paved highways as we know them. Then explain that the story takes place before the invention of cars, when many people rode around in horse-drawn carriages, a very bumpy way to travel. You may also want to mention that many people had only recently moved to the United States from Europe and other parts of the world. Ask students if they have ever ridden on a road full of bumps and holes.

There are some words and phrases in the story that may be new to students. You might wish to briefly explain these words and phrases as you come to them: *moved up in life,* made a success of one's life; *peeved,* annoyed; *a Hoosier porker,* a large pig from Indiana.

GENRE
Historical Nonfiction

A President's Bumpy Ride

By Connie Nordhielm Wooldridge
Illustrated by Nancy Harrison

Bringing the Story to Life

Use a lighthearted tone of voice as you read. Add a dash of sarcasm as you deliver lines like: "calling the thing a 'road' took a lot of imagination" and "the driver had mysteriously disappeared." Increase the urgency in your voice in the paragraph that begins, "Just before 7:00 . . ." To add to the suspense, let out a gasp and pause for a moment just after Mr. Van Buren's carriage crashes.

Americans of the early 1800s loved to move. They moved out, moved on, and moved up in life. They also loved the things that helped them move: things like rivers and canals and, most especially, roads.

On the other hand, they got downright peeved with anyone who kept them from moving. "Stay put" and "know your place" were words many of them had heard in the countries they'd come from, and they weren't about to put up with such talk in America. Martin Van Buren found this out the hard way.

When Mr. Van Buren was president of the United States, a National Road stretched from Cumberland, Maryland, to Vandalia, Illinois. It was the first road ever to be paid for by the United States government. Mail, news, ideas, and people moved along it from east to west and from west back east again.

But to the folks in the Quaker town of Plainfield, Indiana, calling the thing a "road" took a lot of imagination. It was more like an oversized dirt path full of bushes, ruts, and tree roots. A stagecoach ride over it was pure torture. As one passenger put it, "The great object was to prevent our heads coming in contact with the roof of the carriage, when any particularly violent **jolt** threw us with merciless force into the air."

Stagecoach travel was known as "riding the shake-guts."

Why do you think people called it that?

After a hard rain it wasn't uncommon for the coach to get stuck in a mudhole until the driver and passengers could grab some rails from the nearest fence to **pry** the wheels loose. A few miles down the road, they'd have to do the same thing all over again.

The good citizens of Plainfield had a brief moment of hope when Congress passed a bill authorizing road repairs. Their hope didn't last long. The United States was in the middle of a big money crisis, so President Van Buren vetoed the bill.

The people of Plainfield thought about the sorry state of the Road long and hard. They thought about it when they helped vote Mr. Van Buren out of office in the election of 1840. They thought about it for two years after that as they continued to bump and bounce, getting stuck whenever they tried to move from place to place.

Why did the people of Plainfield help vote Mr. Van Buren out of office?

But when word came that on Monday, 13 June 1842, the former president would ride the early-morning mail coach through their very own town to test his **prospects** of running for president again, they started to smile. Some smiled because it was just plain exciting to see a man who used to be president and might be once again—even if you didn't agree with him.

But others smiled for a different reason. The government's money problems were all the way out in Washington, D.C. The Road, on the other hand, ran right through Plainfield. Maybe it was time for Mr. Van Buren to take an up-close look at it.

Just before 7:00 on that particular June morning, the crowd that had gathered spotted the mail coach carrying Mr. Van Buren coming over Davy Carter Hill. As the townsfolk watched it draw closer, they noticed an alarming thing: instead of slowing the horses down, the driver whipped them into a furious gallop. As he neared the giant elm at the edge of town, he pulled on the reins to send the wheels up a bank and over a tree root. The carriage tipped sideways, falling into a mudhole that was deep enough to cover a Hoosier porker up to its neck. For a moment that seemed like forever, not a soul moved.

Finally, Mr. Van Buren's crushed hat, then his head, then the rest of his mud-caked self emerged from the door of the coach that now faced skyward. He was mad; there was no mistake about that. He walked the rest of the way into town. Actually, he didn't have much choice. The carriage sure wouldn't be up and moving anytime soon, and the driver had mysteriously disappeared.

Hmm . . . where do you think the driver went?

The welcoming committee reformed itself into a mop-up crew. With as much courtesy as could be mustered, they got Mr. Van Buren looking polished and presidential again and sent him on his way to Terre Haute, Indiana.

Though Mr. Van Buren never talked about the **incident**, word of it still found its way to Washington, D.C., and got Congress thinking about the Road again in fits and starts.

Why do you think Mr. Van Buren never talked about it?

It took nine long years, but in 1851, a crew finally began the hard work of planking the Road.

The towering elm that silently watched the spilling of a president guarded the spot for many years. That tree saw the muddy ruts of the National Road turn to corduroy, then to gravel, then to cement before it was blown down by a storm in 1929. Today, a newly planted elm marks the same spot. Cars, vans, and buses whiz by on the paved road beside it. It appears as if Americans still like to move out, move on, and move up in life.

And if you ever become president of the United States, you'd best be keeping that in mind!

Talking About the Story

Have students tell why they think the government finally decided to fix the Road. Ask them if they think Mr. Van Buren learned a lesson from his accident.

Encourage students to tell about a time when they thought someone should have listened to them but did not. What happened?

Vocabulary in Action

Words From the Story

jolt

In the story, a stagecoach passenger talked about how a jolt could throw you into the air. If something gives you a jolt, it moves you in a sudden and hard way.

- Ask what would give someone a jolt, getting struck by lightning or sleeping in a soft, warm bed. Explain.
- Have students take turns pretending to receive a jolt.

pry

Stagecoach riders often had to pry the stagecoach wheels out of holes in the road. If you pry something that is stuck, you force it to move or open.

- Ask which thing would have to be pried, a greeting card or a door with a jammed lock. Why?
- Have students pretend to pry something loose from their desk.

prospect

Former President Van Buren took a trip to Plainfield to test the prospects of his being reelected. The prospect of something is the chance that it might happen.

- Ask what has better prospects of happening, finding a cool drink of water in the desert or getting a cool drink of water in a restaurant. Explain why.
- Have students tell about something that has good prospects of happening today.

incident

In the story, Mr. Van Buren never talked about the incident that happened out on the National Road. An incident is an event, usually an unpleasant one.

- Ask which could be called an incident, falling down some stairs or eating a bowl of cereal. Why do you think so?
- Have students talk about an incident they witnessed or heard about.

Vocabulary in Action

Words About the Story

dumbfounded

In the story, the people of Plainfield were shocked into silence by the former president's crash on the road. In other words, the people of Plainfield were dumbfounded by what happened. When you are dumbfounded, you are so surprised that you don't know what to say.

- Ask students when someone might be dumbfounded, after seeing a burning building or after eating a cracker. Why?
- Have students practice dumbfounded expressions.

vindicate

The people of Plainfield were ignored for a long time, but after Mr. Van Buren's accident, the government realized the National Road needed to be fixed. You could say that the people of Plainfield were vindicated. A person who is vindicated is proved to be right after others said they were wrong.

- Ask who is vindicated, a girl who claimed she was innocent and who is proven to have been at a zoo at the time police said she was robbing a bank, or the mailman, by bringing you a package. Explain your answer.
- Have students tell about a time when they or someone they know felt vindicated.

isolated

The town of Plainfield was far away from other towns and cities. Another way to say that is that Plainfield was an isolated town. If something is isolated, it is separate and away from everything else.

- Ask who is isolated, a person at a popular parade or a person alone at their house. Why do you think so?
- Have students find isolated places to stand in the classroom.

refurbish

In the story, a road crew came out and fixed the National Road when it was worn out. In other words, the crew refurbished the Road. If you refurbish something, you make it look like it did when it was new.

- Ask which needs to be refurbished, a beautiful house that was just built or a cabin with a roof that's caving in. Explain.
- Have students name some places or things that they would like to see refurbished.

Helping HOOVES

This informative article tells about Janet and Don Burleson's goal to train miniature horses to be guide animals for the blind.

Vocabulary

Words From the Story

These words appear in blue in the story. Explain these words after the story is read.

navigate **sedate**
phenomenal **mandate**

Words About the Story

Explain these words after the story is read, using context from the story.

astute **humanitarian**
superior **accolade**

Getting Ready for the Read-Aloud

Show students the picture of the miniature guide horse with its vision-impaired owner on page 77. Explain that the guide horse is an alternative to a guide dog. Have students notice the small size of the horse.

Explain that guide animals are very useful for the blind because they act as their owners' eyes. They can help their owners cross streets, walk through crowds of people, and find their way home.

You might want to mention that this article was written in 2001. This means that when the article says "this year" it means 2001.

The following words and phrases occur in the story and can be briefly explained as you come to them: *impaired,* not working correctly; *equine,* horse-like; *defray,* pay for; *recipient,* a person who gets something; *accumulate,* to gather or collect; *without hitches,* without problems; *multiple sclerosis,* a disease that affects the nervous system; *coach section,* the main part of an airplane where people sit.

GENRE
Nonfiction Article

Helping HOOVES

By Michael Neill
and Michaele Ballard

Bringing the Story to Life

Emphasize the surprising facts and ideas in the article, such as the fact that the horses are only 24 inches tall (hold your hand two feet above the floor to demonstrate); that they wear sneakers and diapers; that they guide their owners on elevators and escalators; that they eat popcorn and watch TV with their owners; and that they can ride on airplanes with people.

As she ambles around the Crabtree Valley Mall in Raleigh, N.C., Twinkie is creating quite a stir. Harried shoppers stop in their tracks. Kids gaze openmouthed. After all, you don't get to see a 24-in.-tall miniature horse wearing sneakers (two pairs, for traction) and adult diapers (just in case) every time you head to the store. The green blanket on Twinkie's back explains her presence. It reads: Assistance Animal in Training.

Twinkie, learning the skills she needs to help a blind person around a crowded mall—including **navigating** elevators and escalators—is one of 10 tiny horses being trained at Janet and Don Burleson's 13-acre farm in Kittrell, N.C., outside Raleigh. By later this year, the Burlesons hope to have the horses placed with blind and vision-impaired people around the U.S., to serve as an equine version of guide dogs. "Horses are natural guides," says Janet, 46. "They are extremely calm and they have **phenomenal** memories." The Burlesons, who set up the nonprofit Guide Horse Foundation last May to defray the expenses of acquiring and training the animals (roughly $25,000 each), believe the horses will be especially suitable for vision-impaired people who live in rural areas. "Our goal," says Don Burleson, 44, "is to make them available to the recipients at no cost."

Who are these horses supposed to help?

The couple were newlyweds in 1998 when they bought Smokey, their first miniature horse, as a pet. Soon the clatter of little hooves turned into a mini-stampede, as they added horses the way other people accumulate goldfish. "They are very intelligent, easy to housebreak and incredibly easygoing," says Janet, who began training horses as a teenager. "They come in, eat popcorn and watch TV with us."

It was Twinkie, a silver-dappled mare they acquired in November 1998, who gave them the idea that the horses could be useful to people in need. "When we saw how accessible and eager to work she was," says Don, "we began to realize the possibilities."

Training Twinkie wasn't completely without hitches. "The first time we took her to a grocery store," says Don, "she snapped up a Snickers bar."

Why was it a problem that Twinkie snapped up a candy bar?

In February 2000, after months of training, Twinkie was put to the test at the mall, guiding homemaker and part-time student Karen Clark, 53, of Raleigh, who lost her sight as a child and has already outlived three guide dogs. "On the average, miniature horses live 30 to 40 years," says Don. "A dog's life span is only 10 to 12 years. Mini-horses are also less costly to maintain—they eat grass, maybe $20 a year in oats." And, says Clark, "when we stopped, Twinkie would stand there quietly, where a dog has to sniff everything." In fact, says Janet, the horses are so **sedate** they even take naps while standing in line.

The first guide horses are to go to their new homes in a few months. Among the recipients: Cheryle King, 40, of Gig Harbor, Wash., who lost her sight in 1999 to multiple sclerosis. "I don't think a dog would fit my lifestyle," says King, a former secretary. "I go on trail rides. I think a horse would watch out for my safety better."

And since the Americans with Disabilities Act, which **mandates** that people with guide animals cannot be denied access to public accommodations, makes no distinction between dogs and horses, King will be flying 3-year-old Cricket home with her in style. "She will fly in the front row of the coach section," says Don Burleson. "We've already discussed it with [the airline]. They said that if a passenger is unhappy traveling with an animal, airline personnel will gladly make other arrangements—for the passenger."

Talking About the Story

Have students summarize the story. Ask them what they think about using horses as guide animals.

Ask students whether they'd prefer a mini-horse or a dog to guide them around if they were blind. Why?

Vocabulary in Action

Words From the Story

navigate

In the article, Twinkie helps her owner navigate an escalator and elevator. If you navigate something, you find a way to move on, through, or around it.

- Ask which is an example of navigation, walking through a maze or sitting in a chair. Why do you think so?
- Have students tell about a time they had to navigate something.

phenomenal

Horses have phenomenal memories, according to the story. Someone or something that is phenomenal is unusual because it is so good.

- Ask students which is phenomenal, winning a million dollars or falling down a flight of stairs. Why?
- Have students name something or someone they think is phenomenal.

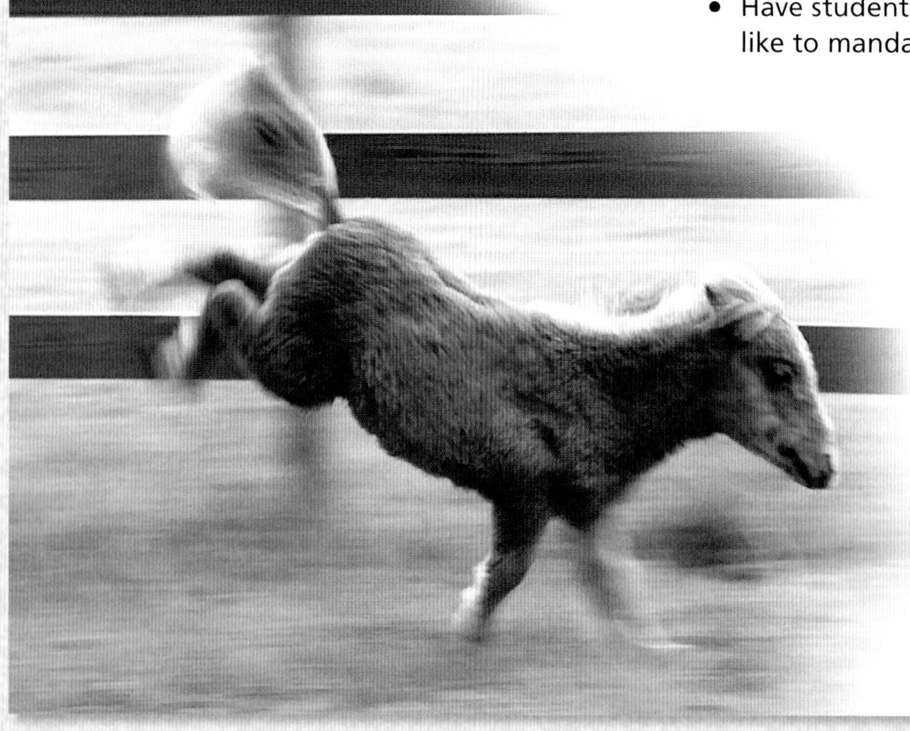

sedate

Mini-horses are very sedate and take naps while standing in line. If a person or animal is sedate, they are quiet and don't get excited easily.

- Ask which should be sedate, a group of people playing football or a group of people in a library. Explain.
- Have students place their hands sedately on their desks for five seconds, then wave their hands wildly in a non-sedate manner for five seconds.

mandate

In the Americans with Disabilities Act it is mandated that people with guide animals have equal access to public places. If you mandate something, you declare it must be done.

- Ask students which is an example of mandating, a parent telling them to put a jacket on before going outside or them getting cold and putting a jacket on. Why?
- Have students say something they would like to mandate.

Vocabulary in Action

Words About the Story

astute

The story says that horses are very smart and have good memories. You could also say that horses are astute. Someone who is astute is very good at understanding things.

- Ask who is astute, a detective who solves crimes or a criminal who gets caught. Why is that?
- Have students tell about a time that they felt astute.

superior

The story says that guide horses are better at their jobs in some ways than guide dogs. The horses are calmer and live longer. You could say that in these ways guide horses are superior to guide dogs. If something is superior, it is far better than something else.

- Ask students which they think is superior, a motorcycle or a bicycle. Why?
- Have students name something that is superior to peanut butter and pepperoni sandwiches.

humanitarian

Janet and Don Burleson train mini-horses to be guide animals for people who are vision-impaired. You could say that Janet and Don are humanitarians. A humanitarian works to improve the lives of people who are suffering.

- Ask students which is a humanitarian act, raising money to help homeless people or saving money to buy a new CD. Why do you think so?
- Have students name something humanitarian that they'd like to do.

accolade

Janet and Don Burleson deserve special recognition for their work to help people who are disabled. You could say they deserve an accolade. If someone is given an accolade, something is done or said about them that shows how much people admire them.

- Ask which is an accolade, going to acting school or getting a Best Actor award for a movie. Explain your answer.
- Have students name some people deserving of accolades.

EGGED ON BY PETE

This is a lively story about a ranch dog named Hank who gets himself into a heap of trouble when he meets up with a wily cat named Pete.

Vocabulary

Words From the Story

These words appear in blue in the story. Explain these words after the story is read.

thrive **surly**
aroma **pulverize**
coordination

Words About the Story

Explain these words after the story is read, using context from the story.

adversary **mortify**
antic

Getting Ready for the Read-Aloud

Show students the picture of a cat tempting a dog with an egg on page 83 and read the title aloud. Explain that the story takes place on a ranch in the western United States. Have them notice the expressions of the two characters: the cat is smug; the dog has an eager look.

Explain that the narrator in this story is actually a dog named Hank and that he is telling a story from his point of view. Explain that he uses regional words and slang expressions to create his very own "voice."

There are some words and phrases in the story that may be new to students. You might wish to briefly explain these words and phrases as you come to them: *brisket,* chest; *gunnysack,* a bag made of rough, heavy fabric; *don't take trash off the cats,* don't let cats insult you; *freeloading,* taking rewards without doing work; *rinky-dink,* unimportant; *snatched him baldheaded,* done him harm; *throwed a hump into his back,* arched his back; *might have made a hand,* might have lent a hand.

GENRE
Fantasy

EGGED ON BY PETE

from *The Further Adventures of Hank the Cowdog*

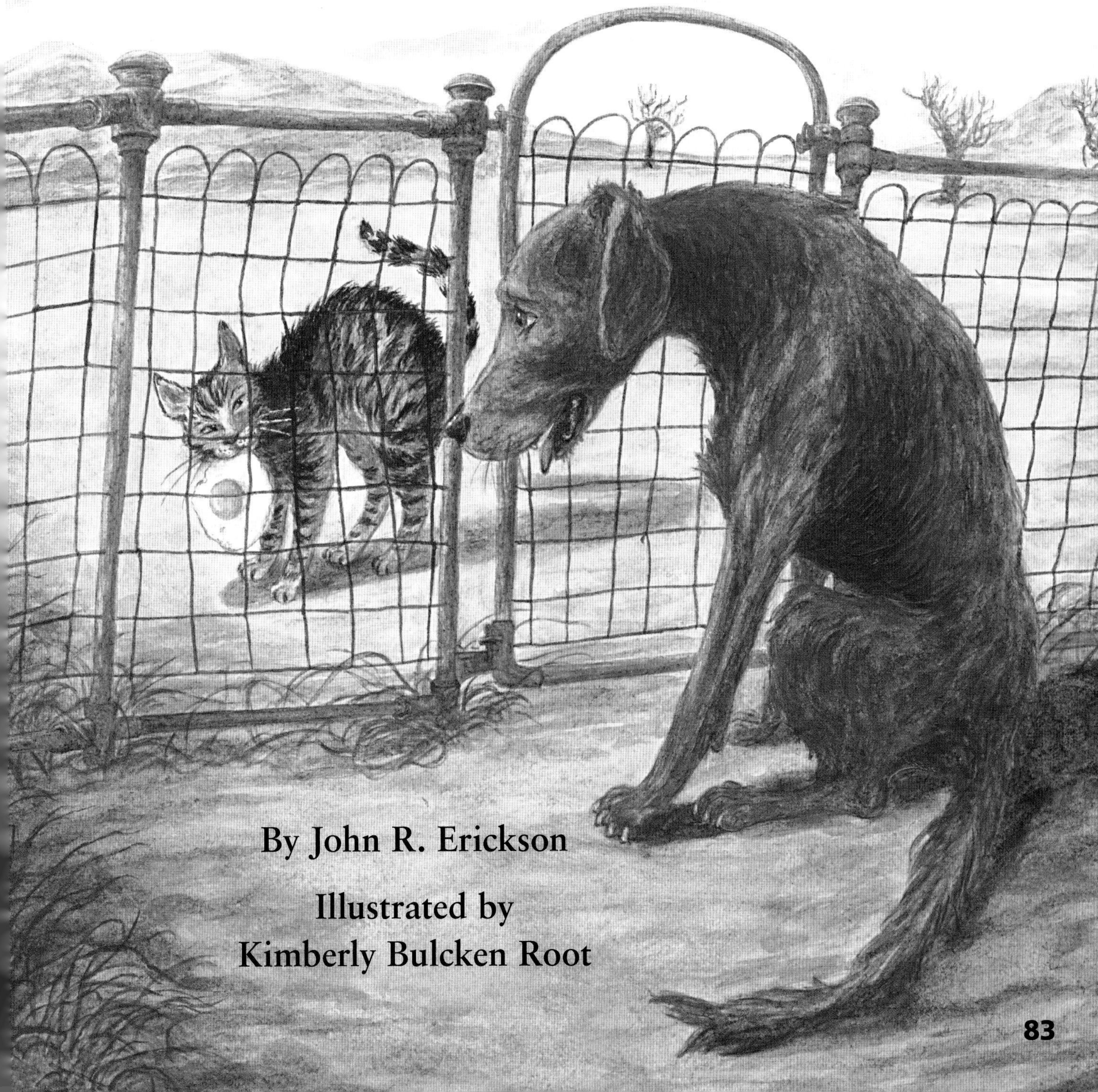

By John R. Erickson

Illustrated by
Kimberly Bulcken Root

Bringing the Story to Life

This story is filled with colorful, regional flavor. Use a "western cowboy" accent and voice for the main character. Display facial expressions that match some of the characters' actions, such as when Drover wrinkles his nose, when Sally May gives Pete a motherly smile and Hank a cold glare, and when Hank growls at Pete.

Hank is not your average dog. No siree-bob; Hank is a smelly, smart-alecky canine detective living on a West Texas ranch owned by Sally May and Loper. As Head of Ranch Security, Hank tackles all sorts of varmints and vandals; but first, he and his junior sidekick Drover must tackle Pete, the lazy, good-for-nothing barn cat.

In the security business, you learn to live your life a day at a time because you never know if you'll make it past that next monster. Any one of them is liable to be your last.

A lot of dogs can't handle that kind of pressure, but there's others of us who kind of **thrive** on danger. When you're in that category, you learn to savor the precious moments. I mean the little things that most dogs take for granted.

Like a roll in the sewer after a big battle. There's nothing quite like it, believe me. You come in hot and bloody and tore up and wore out, proud of yourself on the one hand but just derned near exhausted on the other hand, and you walk up to that pool of lovely green water and . . . well, it's hard to describe the wonderfulness of it.

That first plunge is probably the best, when you step in and plop down and feel the water moving over your body. Then you roll around and kick your legs in the air and let your nose feast on that deep manly **aroma**.

Your poodles and your Chihuahuas and your other varieties of house dogs never know the savage delight of a good ranch bath. If they ever found what they're missing, they'd never be the same again. There's just something about it that makes a dog proud to be a dog.

Well, I climbed out of the sewer and shook myself and sat down in the warm sunshine. Drover was still standing in water up to his knees. I noticed that he hadn't rolled around in it. He never does. He just wades in and stands there, looking stiff and uncomfortable.

How may Drover be different from Hank?

"How do you expect to get clean if you don't get yourself wet?"

He wrinkled his nose. "I don't like to get wet."

"This water has special power, son. It revives the spirit."

He kind of dipped down and got his brisket wet and scampered out on dry land. "There. I feel much better now."

I just shook my head. Sometimes Drover acts more like a cat than a cowdog. Makes me wonder . . . oh well.

We sunned ourselves for a few minutes, then headed on down to the gas tanks. I had a gunnysack bed down there with my name on it and I was all set to pour myself into it. I was fluffing it up again and getting it arranged just right when I heard the back door slam up at the house.

I perked my ears and listened. When the back door slams at that hour of the morning, it often means that Sally May has busted the yoke on Loper's breakfast egg. He won't eat busted eggs, for reasons which I don't understand. Seems to me that an egg's an egg, and after a guy chews it up and swallers it, it's all about the same anyway.

But Loper doesn't see it that way, which is fine with me because around here, in Co-op dog food country, an egg in any form is a gourmet delight.

I cut my eyes toward Drover. He had his chin resting on his front paws and was drifting off to sleep. He hadn't heard the door slam, and I didn't see that it was my duty to tell him about it.

Why doesn't Hank wake up Drover?

I slipped away from the gas tanks and loped up the hill. Had my taste buds all tuned up for a fried egg when I met Pete. He was going the same direction I was.

"Get lost, cat. Nobody called your name."

He gave me a hateful look and hissed. Well, you know me. I try to live by the Golden Rule: "Do unto others but don't take trash off the cats." Pete was in the market for a whipping, seemed to me, so I obliged him. Figgered I might as well get it over with, while it was fresh on both our minds.

I jumped him, rolled him, buried him, cuffed him a couple of times, and generally gave him a stern warning about how cats are supposed to behave. After I'd settled that little matter, I trotted up to the yard gate, ready for my egg.

Do you think Hank will get the egg?

Sally May was standing there with her hands on her hips. I sat down and swept the ground with my tail, gave her a big smile and sat up on my back legs.

I picked up this little begging trick some years ago. It was pretty tough to learn—I mean, it takes balance and **coordination** and considerable athletic ability—but it's paid off more than once. People seem to love it. They like to see a dog beg for what they're going to give him anyway. Don't ask me why, but they do.

Begging sort of goes against my grain. I mean, my ma was no ordinary mutt. She had papers and everything and cowdog pride was sort of bred into me. But a guy has to make a living, and now and then he finds himself cutting a few corners.

Well, I went up on my hind legs. Sometimes I get my balance the first time and sometimes I don't. This time it worked. I balanced myself on two legs, and then to add a special touch, I wagged my tail and moved my front paws at the same time.

I don't believe the trick could have been done any better. It was a real smasher.

I was so busy with the trick that I didn't notice the sour look on Sally May's face. "Hank, you big bully! You ought to be ashamed of yourself for picking on that poor cat!"

Why is Sally May angry at Hank?

"HUH?"

"Just for that, you don't get this egg. Here, Pete, kitty, kitty, kitty."

In a flash, Pete was there. I mean, when it comes to free-loading, he has amazing speed. He gave me a **surly** grin and went through the gate and started eating my egg. That really hurt.

Sally May gave Kitty-Kitty a nice motherly smile, then she turned a cold glare on me. "And besides being a bully, you smell *awful*."

How could she say that? I had just taken a bath, shampooed, the whole nine yards. I mean, a guy can't spend his whole life taking a bath. He's got to get out sometimes and when he does it's just natural that he picks up a few of the smells of the earth.

Besides that, I knew for a fact that Pete hadn't taken a bath in *years*. He hated water even more than Drover did. And he had dandruff too. You could see it all over him, looked like he'd been in a snowstorm.

What kind of justice do you have when a dog that takes a bath every day, and sometimes two or three times a day, gets accused of smelling bad, and a rinky-dink cat . . . oh well.

Pete was chewing my egg, and every now and then he'd turn his eyes toward me and give me a grin. Let me tell you, it took tremendous self-discipline for me to sit there and watch, when all of my savage instincts were urging me to tear down the fence and **pulverize** the cat.

Sally May went back into the house. I should have left right there, just walked away and tried to forget the whole thing. But I didn't.

Pete had laid down in front of the plate. I mean, he was too lazy to stand up and eat. He was purring and flicking the end of his tail back and forth and chewing every bite twenty-three times.

Hank must really want that egg if he's counting how many times Pete chews each bite.

I found myself growling, just couldn't help it. His head came up. "Hmmm, you hungry, Hankie? You'd like this egg. It just melts in your mouth."

"No thanks, I got better things to do." That was the truth. I did. But I stayed there.

Pete shrugged and went on eating. I watched, and before I knew it, I was drooling at the mouth.

Pete got up, took a big stretch, and ambled over to where I was. He started rubbing against the fence. He was so close, I could have snatched him baldheaded, which I wanted to do very sincerely, only there was a wire fence between us.

"I'm not sure I can eat all that egg," he said. "I'm stuffed. You want the rest of it, Hankie?"

I should have said no. I mean, a guy has his pride and everything. But my mouth went to watering at the thought of that egg and . . . "Oh, I might . . . yeah, I'll take it."

He grinned and ambled back to the plate. He picked up the egg in his mouth and brought it over to the fence and dropped it right in front of my nose.

Well, I wasn't going to give him a chance to reconsider, so I made a grab for it. Hit the derned fence with the end of my nose.

But it was right there in front of me. I mean, I could smell it now, it was so close. It was giving off warm waves and delicious smells. I could even smell the butter it had been cooked in.

I made another snap at it, hit the fence and scabbed up my nose. Made my eyes water. When my vision cleared up, I saw Pete sitting there and grinning. I was losing patience fast.

"Gimme that egg. You said I could have it."

"Here, I'll move it a little closer." He got his nose under the egg and nudged it right against the fence.

Well, I just *knew* I could get it now, so I made another lunge for it. Got a taste of it this time, but also wrecked my nose on that frazzling wire. I could see a piece of skin sticking up, right out toward the end.

"Gimme that egg!"

He licked his paw and purred.

Okay, that settled it. I'll fool around and nickel-and-dime a problem for a while, but there comes a time when you've got to get down to brute strength.

Why is Hank still trying to get the egg even though he is hurt?

I backed off and took a run at it and hit the fence with all my speed and strength. I expected at least two posts to snap off at the ground, and it wouldn't have surprised me if I had taken out the whole west side.

Them posts turned out to be a little stouter than I thought, and you might say that the wire didn't break either. The collision shortened my backbone by about six inches and also came close to ruining my nose.

"Gimme that egg, cat, or I'll . . ."

Pete throwed a hump into his back and hissed, right in my face. That was a serious mistake. No cat does that to Hank the Cowdog and lives to tell about it.

I started barking. I snarled, I snapped, I tore at the fence with my front paws, I clawed the ground. I mean, we had us a little riot going, fellers, and it was only a matter of time until Pete died a horrible death.

And through it all, I could still smell that egg, fried in butter.

The back door flew open and Loper stormed out. He had shaving cream on one side of his face and the other side was bright red.

"HANK, SHUT UP! YOU'RE GONNA WAKE UP THE BABY!"

I stopped barking and stared at him. Me? What had I . . . if it hadn't been for the cat . . .

I heard the baby squall inside the house. Sally May exploded out the door. "Will you tell your dog to shut up! He just woke the baby."

"Shut up, Hank!"

Shut up, Hank. Shut up, Hank. That's all anybody ever says to me. Not "good morning, Hank," or "thanks for saving the ranch, Hank, we really appreciate you risking your life while we were asleep." Nothing like that, no siree.

Well, I can take a hint. I gave Pete one last glare, just to let him know that his days on this earth were numbered, and I stalked back to the gas tanks.

I met Drover halfway down the hill. He'd just pried himself out of bed. "What's going on, Hank? I heard some noise."

I glared at him. "You heard some noise? Well, glory be. It's kind of a shame you didn't come a little sooner when you might have made a hand."

"You need some help?"

I glanced back up the hill. Sally May was still out in the yard, talking to her Kitty-Kitty. "Yeah, I need some help. Go up there and bark at the cat."

"Just . . . just bark at the cat, that's all?"

"That's all. Give it your best shot."

"Any special reason?"

"General principles, Drover."

"Well, okay. I'll see what I can do."

What do you think will happen to Drover?

He went skipping up the hill and I went down to the gas tanks to watch the show.

Maybe it was kind of mean, me sending Drover up there on a suicide mission, when he was too dumb to know better. But look at it this way: I get blamed for everything around here, and most of the time I don't deserve it. I figgered it wouldn't hurt Drover to get yelled at once or twice, and it might even do him some good.

Getting yelled at is no fun, but it does build character. Drover needed some character-building. That was one of his mainest problems, a weak character.

So I watched. The little runt padded up to the fence, plopped down, sat up on his back legs, and started yipping. Sally May put her hands on her hips, gave her head a shake, and said, "Well, if that isn't the cutest thing!"

She pitched him my egg and he caught it in the air and gulped it down.

A minute later, he was down at the gas tanks. "I did what you said, Hank, and I won a free egg. Are you proud of me?"

I was so proud of him, I thought about blacking both his eyes. But I was too disgusted. I just went to sleep.

That seems to be the only thing I can do around here without getting yelled at: sleep.

Talking About the Story

Have students tell what they thought about Hank and his actions. Does Hank get what he wants? Why?

Invite students to talk about a time when, if they had behaved differently, things might have turned out better.

Vocabulary in Action

Words From the Story

thrive

In the story, Hank says that he thrives on danger. When someone thrives, they do well and are successful, healthy, or strong.

- Ask which thrives, a houseplant that gets the sun and water it needs or a soccer ball. Explain your answer.
- Have students name things that people need to thrive.

aroma

In the story, Hank rolls in the sewer water and enjoys its "manly" aroma. Something's aroma is how it smells.

- Ask who would probably have a bad aroma, someone who just showered or someone who hasn't showered in a month. Why do you think so?
- Have students show how they would react to the aroma of a freshly-baked cake.

coordination

Hank uses his balance and coordination to perform his begging trick. A person with good coordination can move several parts of their body at the same time without getting mixed up.

- Ask students when you would need great coordination, while walking up some stairs or while trying to perform a ballet dance perfectly. Explain.
- Have students test their coordination by trying to rub their stomachs and pat their heads at the same time.

surly

In the story, Pete gives Hank a surly grin before he starts eating Hank's egg. Someone who is surly behaves in a rude, bad-tempered way.

- Ask what makes you surly, getting encouragement from a friend or getting into an argument with a friend. Why?
- Have students take turns giving a surly look.

pulverize

Hank wants to tear down the fence and pulverize Pete. When you pulverize something, you crush, pound, or grind it into tiny pieces.

- Ask students what could be pulverized, a block of wood or a puddle of syrup. Explain why.
- Have students tell what things in the classroom can be pulverized.

Vocabulary in Action

Words About the Story

adversary

In the story, Hank and Pete are enemies. In other words, they are adversaries. If you are competing against or fighting with someone, they are your adversary.

- Ask who are adversaries, two players on opposite sides of the field or two players on the same team. Why do you think so?
- Have students name some adversaries they know of either from their lives, TV, books, or movies.

antic

Hank's silly behavior gets him in trouble. Another way to say that is that Hank's antics get him in trouble. Antics are funny, silly, or unusual ways of acting.

- Ask students which is an antic, clipping your toenails or wiggling your ears. Explain your answer.
- Have students demonstrate some antics.

mortify

Hank cannot believe that Pete, the cat, got the egg instead of him. In other words, Hank is mortified at the thought of it. If something mortifies you, it offends or embarrasses you a great deal.

- Ask students what would be mortifying, coming to school in your pajamas or dropping a peanut. Why?
- Have students practice looking mortified.

CLOSE ENCOUNTERS

Both the science and the mystique of meteors and comets are brought to life in these tales of close encounters with space rocks.

Vocabulary

Words From the Story & Poem

These words appear in blue in the story and poem. Explain these words after the story and poem are read.

ricochet **radiance**
fragment **dwindle**

Words About the Story & Poem

Explain these words after the story and poem are read, using context from the story and poem.

auspicious **fathom**
fleeting **newsworthy**

Getting Ready for the Read-Aloud

Show students the picture of the boy and ricocheting meteor on page 95 and read the title aloud. Explain that the article tells a true story that took place in a real town on March 26, 2003. Have students notice the look of surprise on the boy's face. Ask them what else they see in the picture. If necessary point out the comet in the sky.

Explain that you will be sharing with them two different types of readings that share a space theme: a nonfiction article and a lyric poem. Discuss how the nonfiction article is based on fact and that the lyric poem is the author's personal expression.

The following terms occur in the story and can be briefly explained as you come to them: *Venetian blinds,* window blinds made up of long, thin slats across a window; *space junk,* trash that spaceships have left up in orbit; *specimen,* a sample.

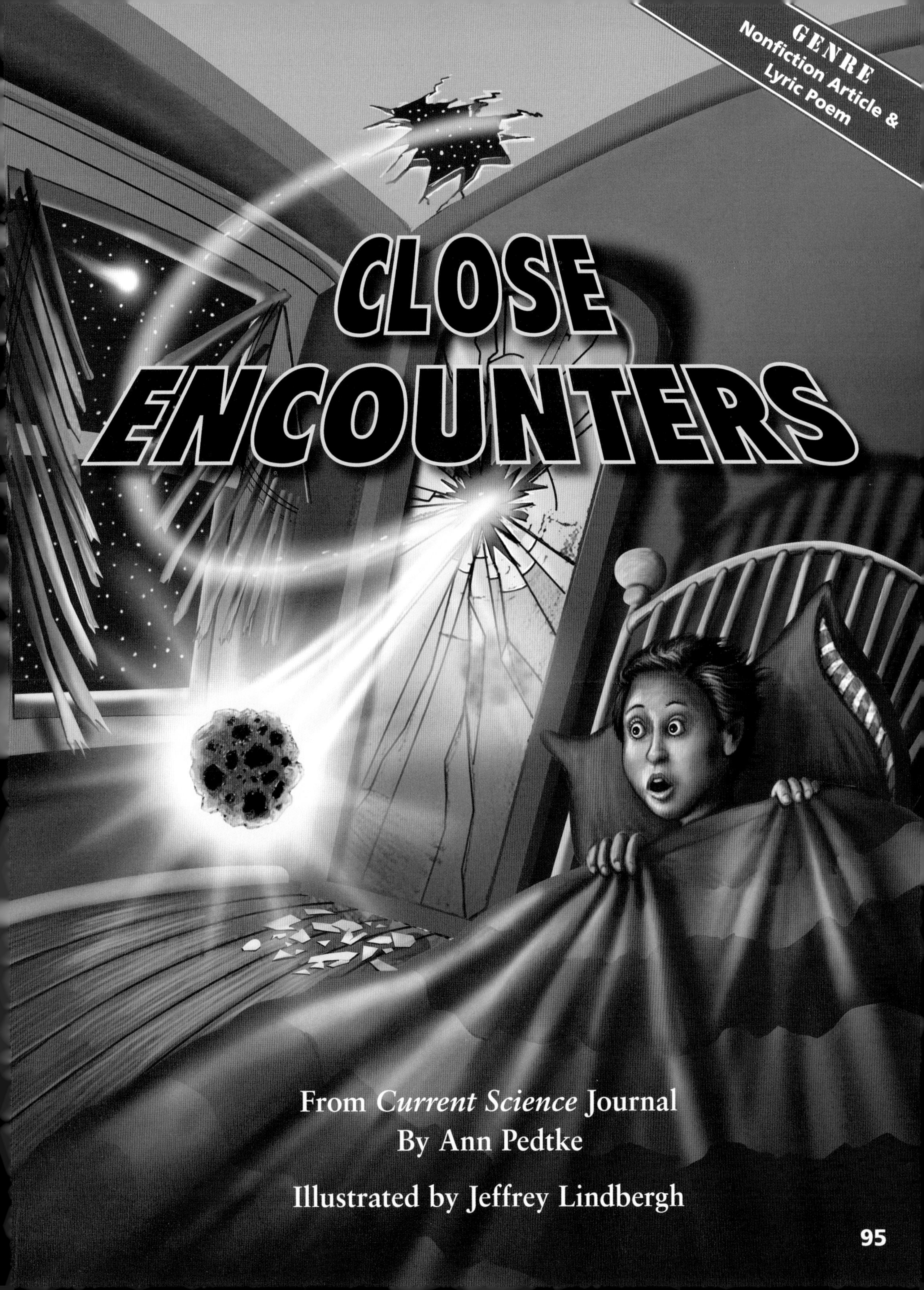

GENRE
Nonfiction Article &
Lyric Poem

CLOSE ENCOUNTERS

From *Current Science* Journal
By Ann Pedtke

Illustrated by Jeffrey Lindbergh

Bringing the Story to Life

Despite the surprising events in the article, this story is true. Avoid giving it too melodramatic a reading. Highlight the excitement of events by emphasizing action words such as "ricocheted," "brilliant fireball," "sonic BOOM," and "hail of rocks."

What would you do if a meteor were flying around your bedroom?

What do you think a sonic boom sounds like?

Space Rock Barely Misses Sleeping Teen

From *Current Science* Journal

Robert Garza, 14, was jolted out of his sleep shortly before midnight on March 26. A softball-sized rock crashed through the roof of his parents' house and **ricocheted** around his room. The rock sliced through a set of Venetian blinds and smashed a floor-to-ceiling mirror before landing on the floor, barely missing the teen.

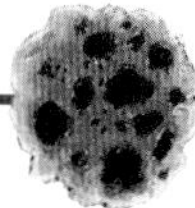

At first, Robert's dad thought the house had been vandalized. Robert's mom had been outdoors and had seen a flash of light in the sky, so she guessed that a piece of space junk had hit the house.

Many residents of the Midwest who were outside that night sighted a brilliant fireball moving northward in the sky. Even more reported the sonic boom that followed. Bright flashes of light came next, followed by a hail of rocks. In the Chicago area, at least six houses and three cars were damaged.

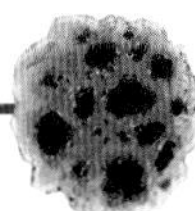

Paul Sipiera, a professor of astronomy at William Rainey Harper College, says the fireball was a meteor, a rocky body from outer space. The sonic boom was the sound of the meteor as it dropped below the sound barrier, and the flashes came from the meteor as it exploded into hundreds of fragments. The **fragments** that hit the ground became meteorites, space rocks that reach Earth's surface without completely burning up.

Did you know that even rocks could catch fire if they are moving fast enough?

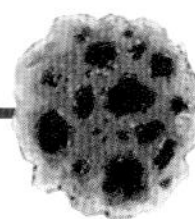

An analysis of the meteorite that hit the Garza home revealed that it is a stony specimen called an ordinary chondrite, a type of meteorite that contains small round granules that once were melted.

The meteor itself probably weighed anywhere from 10 to 25 tons and was about the size of a car, says Sipiera. Meteors of that size hit Earth's atmosphere roughly half a dozen times a year.

Robert Garza no longer has the meteorite that almost hit him. His family sold it to a museum in Washington. "The fact that the meteorite came close to me is pretty cool," Robert told Current Science, "but it didn't really scare me."

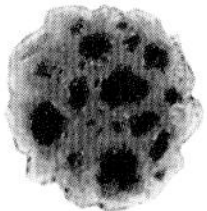

Bringing the Poem to Life

Read the poem in a quiet tone of voice. Remind students that outer space is a very quiet place. Even a comet whirring through space makes no sound. Voice joyful anticipation as the comet approaches the sun and resigned sorrow as it leaves again.

Comet

By Ann Pedtke

A century of darkness,
the sun almost
forgotten . . .
But now, one star grows near,
swelling with brilliance
and heat.
The first shiver
comes, and I can feel
the slow melting begin,
ice shedding,
dust sweeping
behind, as the orbit pulls me in.

Why is the comet melting?

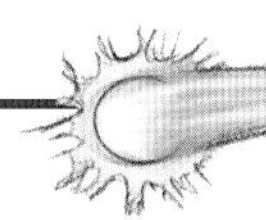

In fiery **radiance**
my existence
dwindles,
yet still I rejoice
in warmth, in light,
granted
for one short
moment
before gravity
releases me
into another hundred years
of night.

Talking About the Story & Poem

Ask students what was similar about the story and poem. Which did they prefer and why?

Ask students if they have ever seen a meteor or a falling star. What did it look like?

Vocabulary in Action

Words From the Story & Poem

ricochet

In the story, the meteor ricochets around Robert Garza's bedroom. When something ricochets, it hits a surface and bounces back from it.

- Ask students which is more likely to ricochet if they throw it at a wall, a tennis ball or an egg. Explain your answer.
- Have students show what a ricochet action looks like by using their hands.

fragment

In the story, the meteor breaks into fragments. A fragment of something is a small piece or part of it.

- Ask which is a fragment, a cookie crumb or a whole cookie. Why?
- Pass around a piece of paper and ask each student to take a small fragment of it.

radiance

In the poem, the comet is described as having fiery radiance. Something's radiance is a glowing light that shines from it.

- Ask what is more radiant, a light bulb or a screwdriver. Why is that?
- Have students name objects in the room that are radiant.

dwindle

In the poem, the comet dwindles as it heats up and melts. If something dwindles, it becomes smaller, weaker, or fewer in number.

- Ask students which dwindles, the amount of milk in their glass during breakfast or water in a river during a heavy rain. Why?
- Have students tell about everyday items that will eventually dwindle.

Vocabulary in Action

Words About the Story & Poem

auspicious

It was a lucky moment when Robert escaped injury by the falling meteor. You could say it was an auspicious moment. Something that is auspicious is a sign that more good things are on the way.

- Ask students which they think is more auspicious, being late to school or finding a dollar on the way to school. Why?
- Have students name some things or events which seem auspicious.

fleeting

In the poem, the comet is only near the sun for a very short moment. Another way to say very short is to say fleeting. If something is fleeting, it only lasts for a short time.

- Ask students which gift has a more fleeting enjoyment, a candy bar that they eat in two minutes or a stuffed animal that they play with for five years. Explain your answer.
- Have students tell about things in their lives that happened in a fleeting moment.

fathom

At first, Robert's parents could not figure out where the noise was coming from. Another way to say that is to say they couldn't fathom where it was coming from. If you cannot fathom something, you can't understand it, no matter how much you think about it.

- Ask which is harder to fathom, the number of stars in the universe or how many days there are in a week. Why do you think so?
- Have students tell some things that are hard to fathom.

newsworthy

The story about the meteor landing on the earth was written in a newspaper because it was interesting to the general public. Another way to say that is to say it was newsworthy. Something that is newsworthy is interesting enough to be reported in newspapers, on the radio, or on television.

- Ask which is newsworthy, the presidential elections or someone eating an apple. Why is that?
- Have students tell which events at school they think are newsworthy.

Prairie Pioneers

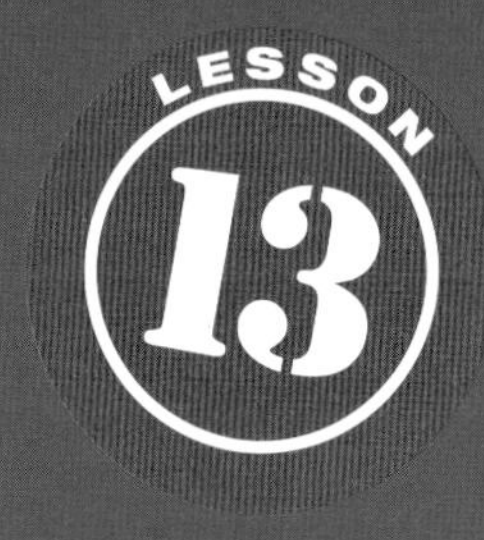

This story describes life in a sod house on the prairie during the pioneer days. You'll read about the hardships that were part of life on the frontier, as well as some advantages to living in a sod house.

Vocabulary

Words From the Story

These words appear in blue in the story. Explain these words after the story is read.

muster
crevice
compact
seldom
scrawl

Words About the Story

Explain these words after the story is read, using context from the story.

repulsive
teem
tolerate

Getting Ready for the Read-Aloud

Show students the picture on page 102 and read the title aloud. Explain that a soddie was a special kind of house that many pioneers lived in during the frontier days of the 1800s. Tell students you will read the story and then the chorus from a popular song about life on the frontier.

Explain that today, most homes are made of wood, brick, or steel. However, there were few trees on the prairie to provide wood, and there were no other building materials handy either. Explain that the pioneers had to build shelters out of the materials that were available. That's why they used sod, or dirt held together by grass roots, to build their homes.

There are some words and phrases in the story that may be new to students. You might wish to briefly explain these words and phrases as you come to them: *acre,* way of measuring land (43,560 square ft., slightly larger than half a football field); *unaccustomed vastness,* unusually large; *warranties,* promise of quality from a seller; *kerosene,* a kind of oil poisonous to bugs.

GENRE
Historical Nonfiction

Prairie Pioneers

By Flo Ota De Lange
By Brewster Higley
Illustrated by Ron Himler

Home, Sweet Soddie

By Flo Ota De Lange

Here you are, a pioneer on the prairie, settled for your first night in your new Home Sweet Home. After you've traveled overland so many miles that it felt as though you'd gone halfway around the world, your straw mattress feels like heaven. But it sure is dark in here. Even though your fingers are right in front of your nose, you can't see them. The dark here is absolutely dark. There are no lights from other houses or from a town or city to reflect on the horizon. Outside there might be stars, but inside there is nothing but the velvety-black black.

So when the first crack of dawn comes, you're anxious to check out your new world. But what's that? It looks like the ceiling above your head is moving. No, it couldn't be. Look again. Now it looks like the wall is moving too. Shut those eyes quick! While you're lying there trying to **muster** your forces to take another look, your parents wake up. Your mother exclaims, "This place is alive with worms!" You look again, and, sure enough, there are worms suspended from the ceiling, worms waving at you from the walls, and—what's that all over the floor? More worms! Hundreds—no, thousands of worms!

Where did all those worms come from? Since there are hardly any trees out on the prairie, the pioneers built their first houses out of sod bricks cut from the surface layer of soil and including all the grasses and roots growing in it. It wasn't easy to build a house of sod. A twelve-by-fourteen-foot shelter required an acre of sod and a great deal of hard work. Because of the thick root system in the prairie grassland, walls built of sod were strong and long lasting. This was one of the advantages. Other advantages of sod houses included the fact that they were better insulated than wood houses, so they were cooler in summer and warmer in winter. They also offered more protection from tornadoes, wind, and fire.

Bringing the Story to Life

Allow your voice to match the mood of each section in the article. For example, when talking about how dark it is, make your voice low and spooky. When talking about the worms, you can sound alarmed. The parts which are particularly gross, like the section about grasshoppers, should be read with great relish and enthusiasm. After the article, you may sing "Home on the Range."

What were the disadvantages? These: Sod blocks were essentially **compacted** soil, which tended to sift down from the ceiling and walls, making it hard, if not impossible, to keep the house clean. Sod also wasn't waterproof. In fact, it was quite the opposite. Whenever there was a heavy rain, water followed the root systems in the sod bricks right on down through the sod ceiling, soaking everything in the room and turning the sod floor to mud. All this dripping didn't stop when the rains stopped either. The roof could leak for days, and that meant people sometimes had to use boots and umbrellas indoors while the sun was shining brightly outside!

Imagine having to use an umbrella inside with the sun shining outside!

The drawbacks of sod houses were not the only difficulties you would have faced as a pioneer on the prairie. Others included the unaccustomed vastness of the wide-open spaces, the endless blue sky, and the almost total lack of neighbors. There were also fleas, flies, mosquitoes, moths, bedbugs, field mice, rattlesnakes, grasshoppers, tornadoes, floods, hail, blizzards, prairie fires, dust storms, and drought. In summer the ground baked, and in winter it froze. The wind blew constantly, and water was as scarce as hens' teeth. One pioneer who couldn't take it anymore left this hardearned lesson **scrawled** across the cabin door of his deserted homestead: "250 miles to the nearest post office, 100 miles to wood, 20 miles to water, 6 inches to misery. Gone to live with wife's folks."

Yes, sirree, homesteading on the prairie was hard work, and there were no warranties on claimed land. The buyers had to take all the risks upon themselves. The term for this arrangement is *caveat emptor*—"let the buyer beware." So what can you do but sweep all those worms out the front door and back onto the prairie? What else can happen, after all?

Well, newly cut sod is home to fleas, and bedbugs come crawling out of it at night. So every morning you have to take your bitten self and your infested bedding out-of-doors and pick off all those bugs. Then you head back inside armed with chicken feathers dipped in kerosene to paint every crack and every **crevice** in every bit of that sod ceiling, wall, and floor.

One creature that doesn't come *out* of the sod, but instead comes *onto* the sod, is the grasshopper. You know, of course, about blizzards of snow. But what about a blizzard of grasshoppers? Enough grasshoppers to block out the sun? So many millions of grasshoppers that they can strip a farm bare in a matter of hours? Did you know that grasshoppers can chew their way through a plow handle? Did you know that grasshoppers are capable of eating almost everything in sight, including fences, bark, and that bedding that you just picked clean of fleas and bedbugs? If a pioneer family had dug 150 feet down for a well—the height of a thirteen-story building—grasshoppers falling into it could sour the water for weeks upon weeks. Grasshoppers could even stop a Union Pacific railroad train from running. Piled some six inches deep on the tracks, their bodies so greased the rails that a train's wheels would spin but not move.

So, welcome to the good life out on the prairie, where "the skies are not cloudy all day." By the way, do you know what constantly blue skies mean for the average farmer?

Actually, blue skies mean there is no rain. No rain means that crops will not grow and that farmers will not be able to eat!

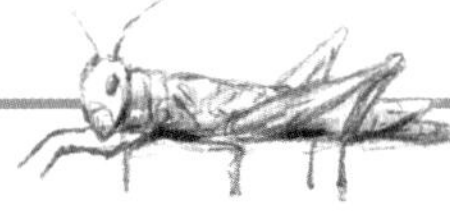

Home on the Range

By Brewster Higley

Home, home on the range,
Where the deer and the antelope play,
Where **seldom** is heard a discouraging word,
And the skies are not cloudy all day.

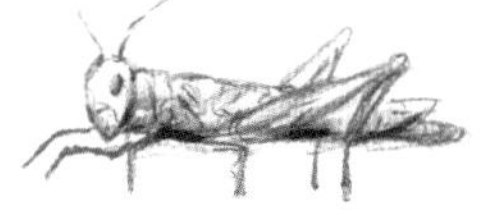

Talking About the Story

Have students tell what was hard about living in a sod house. Does "Home on the Range" paint a different picture of life on the prairie?

Ask students to describe a place that is very different than what they are used to.

Vocabulary in Action

Words From the Story

muster

The story describes how you might have had to muster up enough courage to take another look at the worms. If you muster something, you gather as much of it as you can in order to do something.

- Ask students what they would need to muster, a barber to cut their hair or the strength to move a boulder. Explain.
- Have students tell about a time when they mustered up all of their patience and understanding to keep from getting upset with someone.

compact

Sod houses were made of compacted earth. If you compact something, you press it together to make it smaller or more solid.

- Ask what someone would need to compact, items in a suitcase or a pair of sneakers on the floor. Why?
- Have students compact a piece of paper into as small a ball as they can manage.

scrawl

In the story, a man scrawled a message on the door of his cabin. If you scrawl something, you write it in a careless and messy way.

- Ask which someone might scrawl, a letter to the president or a note to a friend. Explain why.
- Have students use their messiest handwriting to scrawl a sentence on a piece of paper.

crevice

The pioneers spread kerosene into every crevice of their soddie. A narrow crack or gap is called a crevice.

- Ask where you might find a crevice, in a sidewalk or in a milkshake. Explain your answer.
- Have students name things they have seen that have crevices.

seldom

In the song, "Home on the Range," the prairie is described as a place where discouraging words are seldom heard. If something seldom happens, it only happens every once in a while.

- Ask what seldom happens, an earthquake or a sunny day. Why do you think so?
- Have students tell about things that seldom happen.

Vocabulary in Action

Words About the Story

repulsive

Waking up in a house full of worms would be pretty gross! You could say that it would be repulsive. Something that is repulsive is so horrible and disgusting that you want to avoid it.

- Ask students what would be repulsive, having a sandwich for lunch or having a roach for lunch. Explain.
- Have students show what faces they would make if they saw something repulsive.

tolerate

In the story, the pioneers of the prairie had to learn to live in a place where they were not very comfortable. In other words, the pioneers tolerated living on the prairie. If you tolerate something, you accept it even though you don't like it.

- Ask which is something students would tolerate, a visit from their least favorite relative or a visit from the person they most admire. Explain why.
- Have students give examples of situations they have had to tolerate.

teem

The prairie was home to millions of grasshoppers. Another way to say that is that the prairie was teeming with grasshoppers. If a place is teeming with people or animals, it is crowded and the people or animals are moving around a lot.

- Ask students what they would rather receive, a box teeming with puppies or a box teeming with poisonous snakes. Why?
- Have students name various places and what they might be teeming with.

MATTRESSES

In this twist on "The Princess and the Pea," a princess struggles to get a good night's sleep and causes a prince and his mother to think twice about whether or not she would be a good bride.

Vocabulary

Words From the Story

These words appear in blue in the story. Explain these words after the story is read.

dainty **torment**
eloquent **disheveled**
shard

Words About the Story

Explain these words after the story is read, using context from the story.

excruciating **overreact**
fickle

Getting Ready for the Read-Aloud

Show students the picture of the princess on page 109 and read the title aloud. Explain that the princess is frustrated because she cannot sleep. Have them notice the grumpy expression on her face.

Explain that this story is similar to the story of "The Princess and the Pea." Explain that in "The Princess and the Pea," the prince's mother, the queen, places a pea underneath a mattress to see whether or not the princess feels it. The princess does not sleep well because she feels the pea. Only a "true" princess would be able to feel the pea, so she is judged to be fit to marry the prince.

There are some words and phrases in the story that may be new to students. You might wish to briefly explain these words and phrases as you come to them: *down,* very soft feathers; *endure,* put up with; *winced,* moved back as if in pain; *bags under her eyes,* dark, puffy areas under a tired person's eyes.

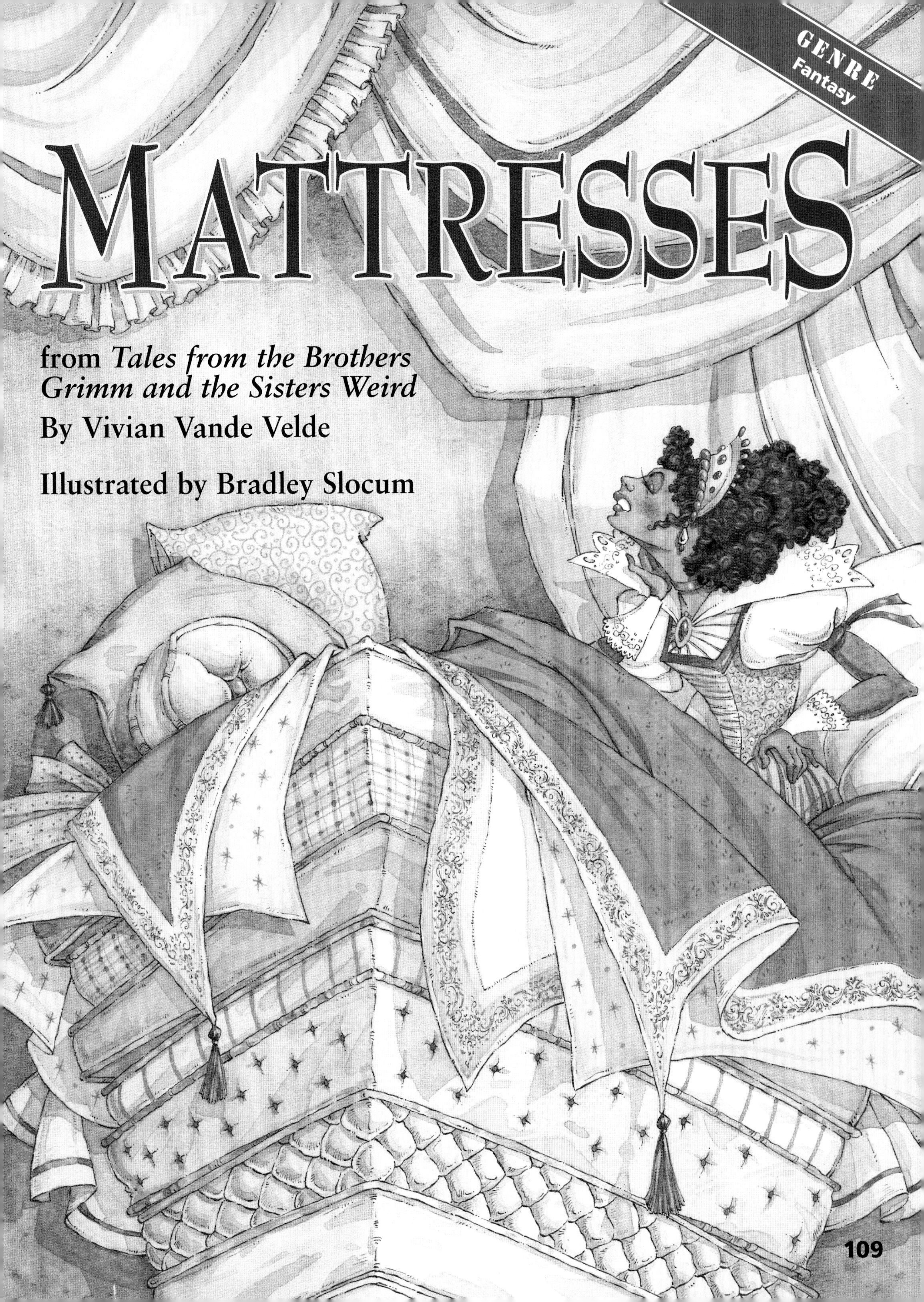

GENRE
Fantasy

MATTRESSES

from *Tales from the Brothers Grimm and the Sisters Weird*

By Vivian Vande Velde

Illustrated by Bradley Slocum

Bringing the Story to Life

As you read the story, emphasize the repetition and the gradual, growing dissatisfaction in the queen's voice. As you read the story, demonstrate phrases such as "with his hand over his racing heart," "crippled by the pain," and "with bags under her eyes." This story invites an impatient tone of voice as it progresses.

Once upon a time, before the invention of waterbeds or air mattresses or adjustable beds, there lived a prince named Royal. Because Prince Royal had such a royal name, great things were expected of him, and when it was time for him to marry, everyone agreed that he needed to find absolutely the most perfect princess to be his wife.

One rainy night while the search for the most perfect princess was still going on, there came a knocking at the door of the castle. The servants opened the door and there stood a most lovely girl, wearing satins and silks and furs, just like a princess, but she was totally drenched, as though she'd been swimming in her fine clothes.

"I am Princess Courtney of Winthrop," she said when she was led into the presence of Prince Royal and his mother, the queen, in the audience chamber. "I've accidentally gotten separated from my traveling companions, and now I'm lost and wet and cold and hungry. May I please spend the night in your castle?"

Prince Royal fell in love immediately. He just stood there, with his hand over his racing heart, unable to remember how to speak. The queen, seeing this, answered graciously, "Of course, my dear," and ordered the servants to prepare a room for Princess Courtney, to find her dry clothes, and to prepare a meal for her.

"Oh my," Prince Royal said as soon as Princess Courtney was escorted from the audience chamber. "Isn't she the most perfect princess you've ever seen?"

"Well," the queen agreed, "she's certainly very beautiful."

Later, at dinner, as the princess ate **daintily**, always knowing which of the several forks and spoons to use, Prince Royal leaned over to his mother and asked, "Isn't she the most perfect princess you've ever seen?"

"Well," the queen agreed, "she certainly has elegant manners."

After that, when Prince Royal had finally remembered how to speak, he and Princess Courtney spoke of politics and philosophy and art.

That night, when Prince Royal stopped by his mother's room to wish her a good night, he sighed and said, "Isn't she the most perfect princess you've ever seen?"

"Well," the queen agreed, "she certainly is very intelligent and **eloquent**."

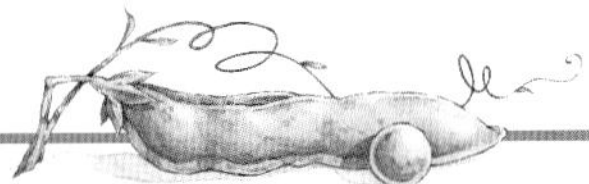

Do you think the prince wants to marry Princess Courtney?

Prince Royal went to bed, planning that in the morning he would ask Princess Courtney to marry him, since she was obviously the most perfect princess in the world. But no sooner had he set his head to his pillow than he heard a loud scream from the princess's bedroom.

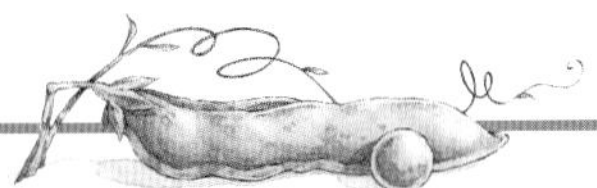

What do you think could be wrong?

The prince, the queen, and all the servants ran to the princess's door. "Courtney, angel," Prince Royal called, "what's the matter?"

Princess Courtney threw open the door and stood leaning weakly against the door frame, one hand pressed to her back.

"What happened?" Prince Royal asked, putting his arm around her because she was obviously shaken.

Princess Courtney pointed to the bed. "That, that . . . *thing*!"

"The bed, my dear?" asked the queen, as though perhaps Princess Courtney had forgotten the word.

"That torture device," Princess Courtney said. "What's the mattress stuffed with?"

The queen went to the bed and pressed against the mattress. "Why, it's stuffed with the down of baby swans, the way all our mattresses are. Do you have allergies?"

"Of course not," the princess snapped. "But your baby swans feel as if they must have rocks and **shards** of glass instead of down. Don't you feel the lumps and bumps and sharp things?"

The queen felt and felt but could find nothing.

Prince Royal hugged Princess Courtney and said, "The most perfect princesses are very delicate."

"Yes," the queen said. "Well, someone go fetch another mattress."

Another mattress was brought and was set upon the first.

"I'm sure that will be much better," Princess Courtney said.

Prince Royal kissed her hand good night and everybody trooped out of the room.

But Prince Royal had no sooner closed the door to his room than he heard a horrible shriek from Princess Courtney's room.

Everybody met once again in front of her door, calling out, "What is it? What's happened?"

Princess Courtney flung open the door, moaning and holding on to her back with both hands this time. "Oh, the anguish, the **torment**!" she murmured.

How do you think they will try to make the princess more comfortable?

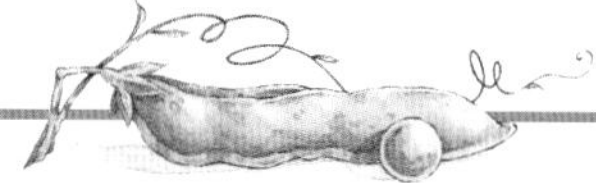

Again the queen felt the bed; again she found nothing wrong. "Bring up two more mattresses," she ordered. "And a step stool so the princess can get up." She patted the princess's shoulder. "There, there," she said. "Four mattresses will make it better."

Princess Courtney smiled graciously.

But once the two additional mattresses were brought and set in place—and once the queen, the prince, and all the servants had stepped out into the hall—the night was once again pierced by Princess Courtney's frantic cries for help.

She came to the door, staggering, her hair wild, her clothes **disheveled**.

Prince Royal patted her hand while the servants went to fetch the five additional mattresses and the stepladder the queen had ordered. "That makes nine mattresses in all," Prince Royal told the princess. "Surely that will be enough."

"If not," Princess Courtney said, "I will try to bear my pain bravely."

As Prince Royal and the queen left the room, Prince Royal whispered to his mother, "She's brave, too. Isn't she the most perfect princess you've ever seen?"

"Well," the queen said, "she certainly is very delicate, even for a princess."

This time Prince Royal not only made it back into his room but even into his bed. He lay his head on his pillow and thought of his brave princess. He yawned. He closed his eyes. He became aware of a sound, not a scream or a shriek or a cry, but a soft whimpering.

Prince Royal got up and knocked on Princess Courtney's door. "Courtney, angel, is everything all right?" He could hear her sobbing.

"Oh, the pain, the pain."

"Courtney, angel, open the door and we'll get you more mattresses."

"I can't," the princess cried. "I've been crippled by the pain."

So Prince Royal had to call for the kingdom's battering ram and twelve strong men-at-arms, who knocked down the door. Prince Royal climbed up the stepladder and lifted the princess off the nine mattresses.

"I tried so hard to be brave," she whispered, "but it was more than my body could endure."

The queen, who had been awakened by the door coming down, ordered ten more mattresses and a full-size ladder.

This time everyone stayed in the room until Princess Courtney was perched on top of her pile of nineteen mattresses. "How is that, my dear?" the queen asked.

Princess Courtney winced but said quietly, "It will do."

In the hallway, Prince Royal turned to his mother.

His mother said, in a tone she'd never used with him before: "Go to bed, Royal."

Do you think the queen is angry and annoyed? How do you know?

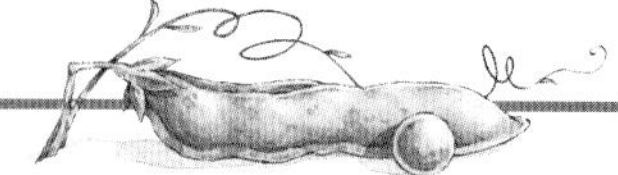

There were no more major disturbances in the night, but all night long they could hear—since the door was gone—the bed springs creaking and the princess sighing.

The next morning, Princess Courtney came to breakfast all stooped over and with bags under her eyes, though she still looked lovely. Actually the queen had bags under her eyes, too, and so did Prince Royal and the servants who were setting out the breakfast.

The queen asked, "Didn't you sleep well, my dear, once there were nineteen mattresses?"

"I tossed and turned all night," Princess Courtney said. "It was as though all those mattresses were perched upon a pointy mountain."

While arrangements were being made for the princess to be returned to her own castle, Prince Royal and the queen went back up to her room. The queen climbed the ladder and lay on the mattresses.

"Do you feel the pointy mountain?" Prince Royal asked.

"No," his mother said. "But then I'm a queen, not a princess."

Still, she ordered the servants to take away all nineteen mattresses so she could examine the bed frame.

What do you think the queen will find? Let's find out.

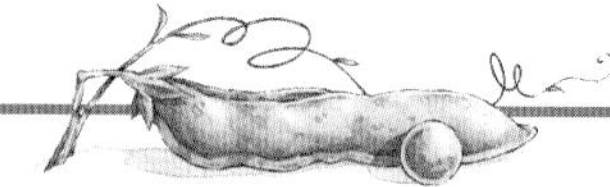

"Ah!" she said.

"Ah?" Prince Royal asked.

The queen picked up a single squashed pea, which had somehow made its way under the first mattress. "This was what she felt."

Prince Royal leaned closer to see. "It's quite small," he said.

"Yes, it is," his mother agreed.

"I guess this shows that Courtney is, indeed, a perfect princess, that she could feel such a tiny thing under all those mattresses."

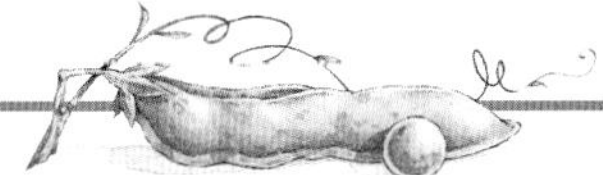

Do you think that the prince will marry the princess?

"It does show that," the queen admitted.

"But it also shows she's very fussy," Prince Royal said.

"Hard to get along with," the queen added.

"Impossible to please," Prince Royal finished.

So they waved good-bye when Princess Courtney set out for home, and Prince Royal never did ask her to marry him.

And after she was gone, everybody went back to bed.

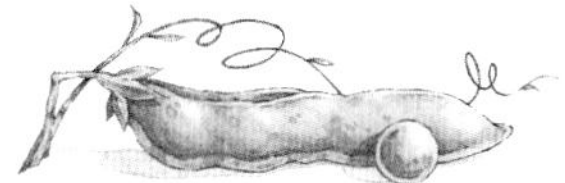

Talking About the Story

Have students tell about their favorite part of the story and explain why they liked it.

Ask students if they or someone they know has ever had trouble falling asleep at night. What did they do to help themselves fall asleep?

Vocabulary in Action

Words From the Story

dainty

In the story, Princess Courtney eats her meal daintily. This means that she eats in a delicate and pretty way, with perfect manners. Dainty can also refer to the way the princess looks and acts. Something that is dainty is delicate, small, and pretty.

- Ask which might be considered dainty, a lion or a flower. Explain.
- Have students give examples of people or things that are dainty.

eloquent

The queen describes Princess Courtney as being eloquent. If you are eloquent, you use words well to say what you mean and get people to think like you.

- Ask when someone might speak eloquently, while giving a speech or while talking to their parrot. Explain why.
- Have students practice speaking eloquently.

shard

Princess Courtney says that sleeping on the mattress is like sleeping on shards of glass. A sharp and pointy piece of broken glass, pottery, or metal is called a shard.

- Ask where you would be more likely to find a shard, at a garbage dump or on a floor that has just been cleaned. Explain your answer.
- Have students tell about a time when they broke a glass or a plate. Did anyone accidentally step on a shard?

torment

In the story, the princess says that sleeping on the mattresses is a torment. If something torments you, it causes you great mental or physical suffering.

- Ask which is a torment, working on a really hard homework assignment or eating ice cream sundaes with your family. Why?
- Have students take turns using body language and facial expressions to show how they feel when they are being tormented.

disheveled

After trying a number of times to get comfortable on the mattresses, the princess's clothes look disheveled. If someone looks disheveled, their hair or clothes are very messy.

- Ask what is more likely to cause you to look disheveled, tucking in your shirt or falling into a puddle of mud. Why do you think so?
- Have students talk about a time when they went out looking disheveled.

Vocabulary in Action

Words About the Story

excruciating

In the story, the princess is in extreme pain while lying on the mattress. You could say that lying on the mattress is excruciating for her. Something that is excruciating is very, very painful.

- Ask which would be excruciating, stepping on a nail or sitting down on a pillow. Why?
- Have students take turns making facial expressions that show excruciating pain.

fickle

Prince Royal seems to be in love with the princess but then changes his mind the next morning after discussing her with his mother. Another way to say that is that he is fickle. If someone is fickle, they change their mind a lot about what they think or want.

- Ask students when they might be fickle, when trying to choose which movie to go to or when eating their favorite food. Explain your answer.
- Have students talk about someone they know who is fickle.

overreact

Prince Royal and the queen think that the princess whined and complained too much. In other words, they think that the princess overreacted. If you overreact to a situation, you respond to it more strongly than you should.

- Ask who might be overreacting to receiving a pencil, someone who says "thank you" or someone who offers to give $200 as a thank-you. Explain why.
- Have students overreact to you giving a homework assignment.

A Day's Wait

This story shows how a child's misunderstanding of temperature scales leads to a bigger misunderstanding of his illness.

Vocabulary

Words From the Story

These words appear in blue in the story. Explain these words after the story is read.

epidemic **evidently**
detach **gaze**

Words About the Story

Explain these words after the story is read, using context from the story.

destiny **presume**
bleak **rebuff**

Getting Ready for the Read-Aloud

Show students the picture of the boy on page 119 and read the title aloud. Explain that the boy is sick with a very high fever. Have them notice the expression on his face.

Explain that this story is based on a real-life experience that writer Ernest Hemingway had with his son, Bumby. Ask students to share what they know about having a fever. Have them talk about how they felt when they last had a fever and who took care of them while they were sick. Ask them if they remember how high their temperature was.

The following phrases occur in the story and can be briefly explained as you come to them: *purgative,* a medicine that helps the body get rid of mucus or vomit; *influenza,* a sickness also known as the flu; *flushed a covey of quail,* startled a group of birds into leaving the bushes.

GENRE
Nonfiction Narrative

A Day's Wait

By Ernest Hemingway
Illustrated by Ron Mazellan

Bringing the Story to Life

Read the dialogue aloud with different voices for Hemingway and his son. Portray Hemingway as relaxed and only mildly concerned while Schatz's voice is very solemn. Demonstrate taking Schatz's temperature to make this story more vivid.

To understand this story, you have to know that there are two kinds of thermometers, each using a different temperature scale. On the Celsius thermometer, used in Europe, the boiling point of water is 100 degrees. On the Fahrenheit thermometer, used in the United States, the boiling point is much higher, 212 degrees.

The events in this story really happened to Ernest Hemingway and his nine-year-old son Bumby. (In this story, Bumby is called Schatz, a German word meaning "treasure.") Hemingway and his family lived in France for many years; in this story they are back in the United States.

He came into the room to shut the windows while we were still in bed and I saw he looked ill. He was shivering, his face was white, and he walked slowly as though it ached to move.

"What's the matter, Schatz?"

"I've got a headache."

"You better go back to bed."

"No. I'm all right."

"You go to bed. I'll see you when I'm dressed."

But when I came downstairs he was dressed, sitting by the fire, looking a very sick and miserable boy of nine years. When I put my hand on his forehead I knew he had a fever.

"You go up to bed," I said, "you're sick."

"I'm all right," he said.

When the doctor came he took the boy's temperature.

"What is it?" I asked him.

"One hundred and two."

Is that a very bad fever?

Downstairs, the doctor left three different medicines in different-colored capsules with instructions for giving them. One was to bring down the fever, another a purgative, the third to overcome an acid condition. The germs of influenza can only exist in an acid condition, he explained. He seemed to know all about influenza and said there was nothing to worry about if the fever did not go above one hundred and four degrees. This was a light **epidemic** of flu and there was no danger if you avoided pneumonia.

Back in the room I wrote the boy's temperature down and made a note of the time to give the various capsules.

"Do you want me to read to you?"

"All right. If you want to," said the boy. His face was very white and there were dark areas under his eyes. He lay still in the bed and seemed very **detached** from what was going on.

I read aloud from Howard Pyle's *Book of Pirates;* but I could see he was not following what I was reading.

"How do you feel, Schatz?" I asked him.

"Just the same, so far," he said.

I sat at the foot of the bed and read to myself while I waited for it to be time to give another capsule. It would have been natural for him to go to sleep, but when I looked up he was looking at the foot of the bed, looking very strangely.

"Why don't you try to go to sleep? I'll wake you up for the medicine."

"I'd rather stay awake."

Why do you think Schatz doesn't want to go to sleep if he's sick?

After a while he said to me, "You don't have to stay in here with me, Papa, if it bothers you."

"It doesn't bother me."

"No, I mean you don't have to stay if it's going to bother you."

I thought perhaps he was a little lightheaded and after giving him the prescribed capsules at eleven o'clock I went out for a while.

It was a bright, cold day, the ground covered with a sleet that had frozen so that it seemed as if all the bare trees, the bushes, the cut brush, and all the grass and the bare ground had been varnished with ice. I took the young Irish setter for a little walk up the road and along a frozen creek, but it was difficult to stand or walk on the glassy surface and the red dog slipped and slithered and I fell twice, hard. . . .

We flushed a covey of quail under a high clay bank with overhanging brush . . . Some of the covey lit in trees, but most of them scattered into brush piles and it was necessary to jump on the ice-coated mounds of brush several times before they would flush. . . . [I] started back pleased to have found a covey close to the house and happy there were so many left to find on another day.

At the house they said the boy had refused to let anyone come into the room.

"You can't come in," he said. "You mustn't get what I have."

Why won't Schatz let anyone in his room?

I went up to him and found him in exactly the position I had left him, white-faced, but with the tops of his cheeks flushed by the fever, staring still, as he had stared, at the foot of the bed.

I took his temperature.

"What is it?"

"Something like a hundred," I said. It was a hundred and two and four tenths.

"It was a hundred and two," he said.

"Who said so?"

"The doctor."

"Your temperature's all right," I said. "It's nothing to worry about."

"I don't worry," he said, "but I can't keep from thinking."

"Don't think," I said. "Just take it easy."

"I'm taking it easy," he said and looked straight ahead. He was **evidently** holding tight onto himself about something.

"Take this with water."

"Do you think it will do any good?"

"Of course it will."

I sat down and opened the *Pirate* book and commenced to read, but I could see he was not following, so I stopped.

"About what time do you think I'm going to die?" he asked.

"What?"

"About how long will it be before I die?"

"You aren't going to die. What's the matter with you?"

"Oh, yes, I am. I heard him say a hundred and two."

"People don't die with a fever of one hundred and two. That's a silly way to talk."

"I know they do. At school in France the boys told me you can't live with forty-four degrees. I've got a hundred and two."

He had been waiting to die all day, ever since nine o'clock in the morning.

"You poor Schatz," I said. "Poor old Schatz. It's like miles and kilometers. You aren't going to die. That's a different thermometer. On that thermometer thirty-seven is normal. On this kind it's ninety-eight."

"Are you sure?"

"Absolutely," I said. "It's like miles and kilometers. You know, like how many kilometers we make when we do seventy miles in the car?"

"Oh," he said.

But his **gaze** at the foot of the bed relaxed slowly. The hold over himself relaxed too, finally, and the next day it was very slack and he cried very easily at little things that were of no importance.

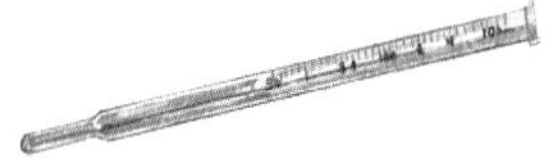

Talking About the Story

Have students describe what they liked about the story.

Ask students about a time when they were sick. Did they worry about anything?

Vocabulary in Action

Words From the Story

epidemic

In the story, the doctor says that there is an influenza epidemic. If there is an epidemic of something, it affects a large number of people and spreads quickly.

- Ask which is an epidemic, two children with hula hoops or a whole town of people playing with yo-yos. Explain your answer.
- Have students pretend a smile epidemic just swept through the classroom.

detach

In the story, Schatz is detached from what is going on. If you detach something, you remove or separate it from another thing. Someone who is detached from a situation is acting as though they are separate from it and it does not affect them.

- Ask students which would make them feel more detached, something happening to their family or something happening to a strange character in a movie. Why?
- Have students list some things they are detached from and some things they are not detached from.

evidently

Hemingway writes that Schatz was evidently holding tight onto himself about something. If something is evidently true, there is proof that it is true.

- Ask students which is more evidently true, that it gets dark at night or that there's a monster under their beds. Why is that?
- Have students give examples of things that are evidently true.

gaze

Schatz's gaze relaxed after he realized that he wasn't going to die. Someone's gaze is how they are looking at something, especially when they are looking steadily at it.

- Ask who is gazing at something, the person who spends long minutes admiring the stars in the night sky or the person who quickly checks the sky for clouds before getting dressed for the day. Explain.
- Have students gaze at various things around the room.

Vocabulary in Action

Words About the Story

destiny

In the story, Schatz believes that he has no choice but to die of influenza. Another way of saying that is that his destiny is to die of influenza. If something is your destiny, it will happen to you and you cannot change it.

- Ask students which is their destiny, to grow up or stay the same age they are now. Why do you think so?
- Ask students what they think their destinies are.

bleak

Schatz is convinced that his outlook is not hopeful. Another way of saying something is not hopeful is to say it is bleak. If a situation is bleak, it is bad and unlikely to get better.

- Ask which is bleak, a bright June day or a cold, gray, windy November afternoon. Explain your answer.
- Have students name some things that they think are bleak.

presume

In the story, Schatz jumps to the conclusion that he will die. You could say he presumes he will die. If you presume that something is so, you think it is so, but you are not sure.

- Ask students which is an example of presuming, meeting a new classmate and asking her name or seeing a new classmate and deciding right away they will not be friends. Why?
- Ask students whether they have ever presumed something. Were they proved right or wrong in the end?

rebuff

Schatz refuses to allow anyone to visit his bedroom. You could say he rebuffs all his visitors. If you rebuff someone, you rudely refuse them and make them go away.

- Ask students who is rebuffing them, the person who returns their smile or the person who ignores them. Explain.
- Have one volunteer suggest something and have another volunteer rebuff the idea.

The Merchant's Camel

This humorous story is an ancient legend from the Islamic culture. Find out what happens when a man who has lost his beloved camel crosses paths with some ministers who can describe the camel suspiciously well.

Vocabulary

Words From the Story

These words appear in blue in the story. Explain these words after the story is read.

possession **scarcely**
venture **keen**

Words About the Story

Explain these words after the story is read, using context from the story.

scrutinize **elucidate**
quandary **plentiful**

Getting Ready for the Read-Aloud

Show students the picture of the four ministers on page 127 and read the title aloud. Explain that they are describing the merchant's lost camel and that the images in the clouds show what they are saying about how the camel looked. Have students guess what the camel may be like.

Explain that this story is a folktale, or a well-known story, that has been passed down over time. Tell students that the story is set in India and that the main characters are a merchant and four ministers. Then let them know that a merchant is someone who sells goods and that the ministers are government advisors.

There are some words and phrases in the story that may be new to students. You might wish to briefly explain these words and phrases as you come to them: *the cow and the jaguar drank side by side at shady pools, and the butterfly and snake laid eggs in the same nest,* things were so peaceful that predators and prey got along; *lame,* unable to walk without difficulty; *abundant,* a large amount.

GENRE
Indian Folktale

The Merchant's Camel

from *The Spectacular Gift and Other Tales from Tell Me a Story*

Retold by Amy Friedman

Illustrated by Jillian Gilliland

Bringing the Story to Life

Read the dialogue using interesting and distinct voices for the four wise ministers. Capture the frustration and desperation of the merchant through the tone of your voice, facial expressions, and body language. As you read, demonstrate each of the camel's characteristics as they are described by the wise ministers.

Once upon a time a great king ruled over a prosperous land. The king was known far and wide for his wisdom and generosity, and all the people of his land loved him. During this good king's reign, the cow and the jaguar drank side by side at shady pools, and the butterfly and snake laid eggs in the same nest. When the land was dry, rain fell, and when the fields were thick with mud, the sun burst through the clouds and dried the earth. Flowers and plants blossomed and bloomed.

Now one day a merchant lost his prize **possession**, his favorite camel. He searched high and low, day after day, for the beast. Alas, after weeks of having no luck, he **ventured** out across the borders of the land. "Perhaps she has wandered far away," he said to himself, and off he went.

After some days he came upon four men walking in the opposite direction. "Hello there," said the merchant, as he crossed the men's path. "Where do you travel?"

"We are unhappy men," said the first man. "We are ministers in our own land, but our land is ruled by a cruel and unjust king. We have decided to seek another place to live."

"I see," said the merchant.

"And you?" they asked. "Why is it you are wandering?" the first minister asked.

"I have lost my poor camel," said the merchant. "I am off to see if I can find her somewhere in this great, wide world. Have any of you seen a camel in your journeying? I doubt it, of course, and soon I think I will give up my search."

The ministers gathered together. They bowed their heads and spoke together in whispers. The merchant stood nearby. He leaned forward to try to hear what the men said.

What do you think the ministers are saying? Do they know where the camel is?

"Have you seen her?" he asked again. "Tell me what you whisper about."

"I wish to ask you something, kind sir," said the first minister.

"Anything," said the merchant. His heart began to beat faster, for the four men seemed to be wise.

"Was your camel lame, good sir?" the first minister asked.

"Yes, she was!" cried the merchant. Now he was truly excited. "Yes, yes! Where have you seen my camel?"

But the first minister simply closed his eyes and fell silent, and the second minister stepped forward to speak. "And was your camel blind in one eye?" he asked.

"Oh, yes!" cried the merchant. "She was blind and lame, but such a good creature. Oh, won't you tell me where you have seen my camel?" But at that the second minister fell silent and closed his eyes.

The third minister stepped forward. He touched his hand to the merchant's shoulder and said softly, "Tell me, was your creature's tail unusually short?"

"Stop teasing me!" shouted the merchant. "Tell me where you saw my camel!"

But the third minister closed his eyes, and the fourth minister stepped forward. He bowed low and spoke as softly as his friends. "I believe your camel may have had a cough. Could that be so?"

"I have been teased enough!" the merchant wept. "You men are cruel, for you know everything about my poor lost camel. Tell me now where my creature has gone."

"I am so sorry," said the first minister, "but none of us has seen your camel anywhere."

Do you believe the ministers? Do they really not know where the merchant's camel is?

"You play with me!" cried the merchant.

The second minister smiled gently. "We do not tease or play," he said. "None of us has seen your camel. We have only observed her."

"What can you mean?" cried the merchant.

"Follow us," said the four ministers. "We are on our way to your land to see your king. Let him explain to you what we have discovered on our journey."

"I am certain you have stolen my animal," hissed the merchant, "and now you ask me to go home, defeated and without my finest possession."

The ministers smiled again. "Come with us," they urged the merchant, and at last, lost and sad, he fell silent and followed the four ministers to his land.

The five men approached the castle. "Here I will find justice," said the merchant. "Our ruler is a kind man."

"That is what we hope," said the ministers, and all five men appeared before the king.

"Tell me what it is you need," said the king.

Quickly the merchant told the king of the men's findings. "I believe they have stolen my camel," he said.

The king sat up straight. "You have described this creature perfectly," he said. "Tell us how it is you know all about the camel."

The first minister bowed to the king. "Good sir, when I first saw the creature's tracks, I noticed that one of the footmarks was deeper than the others. That is how I knew she must be lame."

"And I," said the second minister, "observed that the leaves on one side of the road were snapped, while the others grew abundant and green. I knew then that the animal was blind in her left eye, for clearly she did not see the fruits of the trees on the left."

"I see," said the king. "And you?" he asked, turning to the third minister. "How did you know that the creature's tail was short?"

"Upon the road I saw small drops of blood," said the third minister. "And I realized that the flies and gnats had bitten her, but her tail was too short to shoo them away."

"Ahh," said the king, smiling, then turning to the fourth minister. "And you, sir, how could you know of the camel's illness?"

"I observed the footprints and saw that the hind leg prints **scarcely** touched ground," said the fourth minister. "And so I knew that the camel must have contracted in pain."

"Ah," said the king, and then he turned to the merchant and said, "I will pay for the loss of your camel as she seems to be lost for good. And you," said the king, turning to the ministers, "please stay and be my counselors, for you are observant, **keen** and wise."

Why does the king want the ministers to stay and be his counselors?

And so the four ministers came to help the great king of India. The merchant gathered all the people and praised their good king and the wise ministers.

There is an ancient saying in Islam: "Faith is the lost camel of the Believer." Some people say that this phrase originates from this tale, the lost camel representing man's faith, its traces visible only to those who observe carefully and use their power wisely.

Talking About the Story

Have students summarize what happened in the story and tell whether they were surprised that the ministers had not stolen the camel.

Ask students if they have ever lost something that was important to them. Did they find it? How?

Vocabulary in Action

Words From the Story

possession

In the story, the merchant is searching for his most valuable possession, his camel. Your possessions are the things you own.

- Ask which is a possession, a library book or the shirt you are wearing. Why?
- Have students hold up various possessions they have with them.

venture

The merchant ventures outside of the land where he lives when he leaves to look for his camel. If you venture somewhere, you go somewhere even though it might be dangerous.

- Ask where someone might venture, into the forest to rescue a hurt animal or into a classroom to paint a picture. Explain your answer.
- Have students talk about exciting places they might like to venture.

scarcely

The fourth minister says that the camel's footprints showed that its hind legs scarcely touched the ground when it walked. You use scarcely to say that something is just barely the case.

- Ask students where there is scarcely any water, in an ocean or in the desert. Why do you think so?
- Have students use facial expressions and body language to show how they act when they can scarcely contain their excitement.

keen

The king wants the four ministers to stay in his land to become his counselors because they are keen and wise. If someone is keen, they are very aware and able to see even the most minor details.

- Ask who might be described as keen, a person who sees a giraffe in the street or a person who sees an old penny on the street. Explain.
- Have students practice being keen by giving detailed descriptions of classroom items.

Vocabulary in Action

Words About the Story

scrutinize

The ministers know certain things about the camel because they carefully observed the path. In other words, they scrutinized the path. When you scrutinize something, you look at it very closely and carefully.

- Ask students who would be scrutinizing, someone checking out a flat bicycle tire that was full of air yesterday or someone glancing at a plastic bottle that was full of soda yesterday. Explain why.
- Have students take turns scrutinizing a sentence with a small spelling error.

quandary

After hearing what the ministers had to say about his camel, the merchant wants to follow them and see the king, but he does not want to stop looking for his camel. In other words, he is in a quandary. If you are in a quandary, you have to make a decision but can't decide what to do.

- Ask when you would be in a quandary, if you really wanted to eat a piece of strawberry cake but were allergic to strawberries or if you really wanted some brownies and your mom baked some for you. Why?
- Have students tell about a time when they have been or might be in a quandary over something.

elucidate

In the story, the four wise ministers explain their observations to the king. Another way to say that is that they elucidate the details of the story. If you elucidate something, you make it clear and easy to understand.

- Ask when you might elucidate, when giving a friend directions to your house or when giving a friend a piece of gum. Explain.
- Have students tell about a time when they elucidated something for a friend.

plentiful

When the ministers talk to the king, they explain that there were many clues along the road that made it possible for them to describe the camel. Another way to say that is that the clues about the camel were plentiful. If something is plentiful, there is so much of it that there's enough for everyone.

- Ask what might be plentiful on a farm, space shuttles or tomatoes. Why do you think so?
- Have students describe some things that might be plentiful, either in their lives or in our country.

Skeleton Barrels Back into Olympics

This nonfiction article is about a little-known sport called skeleton. The story describes the lure of the sport, its history, and the trailblazing way today's athletes have brought the sport to the world's attention as part of the Olympic Games.

Vocabulary

Words From the Story

These words appear in blue in the story. Explain these words after the story is read.

skim **subtle**
insistent **maneuver**
unscathed

Words About the Story

Explain these words after the story is read, using context from the story.

intense **fanatical**
audacious

Getting Ready for the Read-Aloud

Show students the picture on page 135 and read the title aloud. The photograph shows an athlete performing in an Olympic sport that they might not have heard of before—skeleton.

Explain that skeleton is a winter sport using a sled to slide very fast over a steep, curving track made of ice. Ask students if they have ever seen a sled race. Explain that the difference between skeleton and other sledding sports like bobsled or luge is that the racer goes head first rather than feet first. 2002 was the first time in over fifty years that skeleton was at the Olympics.

There are some words and phrases in the story that may be new to students. Briefly explain these expressions as you come to them: *swerves and straightaways,* sharp turns and straight passages; *stream of consciousness,* telling events as they are perceived without taking time to order them into a story; *a locomotive,* a train; *kamikaze style,* so dangerous it seems suicidal; *physics,* the branch of science that explores motion; *Rosetta Stone,* a carved stone the discovery of which led to several breakthroughs in understanding ancient cultures; *comic relief,* an amusing distraction.

GENRE
Nonfiction Article

Skeleton Barrels Back into Olympics

By Mark Sappenfield

Bringing the Story to Life

Read the story dramatically and project a high level of energy in your voice and body movements when describing the speed and danger of this sport. Read the narration with the reporter's tone of astonished awe. Speak the quotes with the intense tone of the athletes. Say "like any normal human being" with ironic humor.

What kind of person do you think would enjoy this sport?

Sitting in a room with America's five Olympic skeleton sliders, the question inevitably arises: So what is it like careening down the swerves and straightaways of a bobsled track, head first, feet flailing?

A few try to explain it, and stream of consciousness comments ensue—as fast and dizzying as a gold-medal run. In the end, each concludes, "it's like nothing else."

Finally, Lincoln DeWitt, last season's World Cup champion, offers a colleague's assessment: Imagine driving down a highway at 85 mph., then opening the door and sticking your head out so it nearly **skims** the asphalt.

The others nod, and you get the feeling that if that were an organized sport, they might give it a try, too. Today, skeleton arrives as the Olympics' newest sport, and its cast of characters is among the Games' most engaging. Perhaps that's no surprise, given the kind of person it takes to hop onto a three-foot-long (one-meter) sled and accelerate to the speed of a locomotive—all while your chin hovers two inches (five centimeters) off the ice.

There is Lea Ann Parsley, the 1999 Ohio firefighter of the year, who saved a mother and daughter from a burning building and is currently pursuing her Ph.D. in nursing. There is Chris Soule, who worked as a stuntman in the film *G.I. Jane,* and counts cliff diving among his past exploits. And there is Jim Shea, the third-generation Olympian who switched from bobsled, in part because he felt—like any normal human being—that it was just too boring.

All say they don't think of themselves as daredevils. Instead, they are missionaries for a sport that was actually a predecessor of bobsled and luge, yet for decades has been all but forgotten by all except a few enthusiasts ensconced deep within the Alps. Now, more than 50 years after it last appeared in the Olympics, it returns as—in some ways—the Games' ultimate thrill ride.

"Everyone has to take at least one run in their lives," says Tristan Gale, more animated and **insistent** than a grade schooler throwing a slumber party. "You will experience something you have never done before. You finish, and your eyeholes are huge. It takes days to process it."

Watch one run, and the allure of skeleton is obvious: it's kamikaze style. Although luge is fractionally faster, the fact that skeleton sliders go down head first with no steering mechanism has given it a reputation as the crazy uncle of sliding sports. To some degree, the reputation is warranted.

Shea recounts tales of broken noses and punctured lungs. Parsley, who read about the sport on the Web and had never actually seen it before she took her first run, once applied shoe glue to her face so she wouldn't have to go to a hospital to stitch a cut. Soule wrapped himself in duct tape so his sweater wouldn't be ripped off when he hit the walls.

This is dangerous!

Indeed, in earlier days, when today's Olympians were new to the sport, skeleton seemed as much a dare as a technical discipline. Technique was an ongoing experiment; steering was an afterthought. Merely making it through a run **unscathed** was a victory in itself.

"I remember looking up and seeing how much speed I'd gained," says DeWitt about his first run. "The turn looked like a wall, and I remember thinking, 'I have no concept of the physics of what is about to happen.'" At the end, though, undaunted, "I asked if I could get a refund on my season ski pass, because I knew I wasn't going skiing anymore."

Why did DeWitt give up skiing?

When he talks about his sport now, it's as if he's speaking of the Rosetta Stone—an artifact that has been unearthed, studied, and is only now starting to be comprehended.

Invented by British tourists in St. Moritz, Switzerland, in 1884, skeleton is considered the first organized sliding sport. The first bobsled was simply two skeletons lashed together.

An earlier form of skeleton was a part of the two St. Moritz Winter Games—in 1928 and 1948—with Americans taking three of the six medals.

But over generations, the science of skeleton was lost in the haze of history. The sport faded entirely from North America and clung only to a few European clubs in countries such as Germany, Austria, and Switzerland. Even the origin of the name "skeleton" was lost—although most believe it comes from the fact that the early frame sleds looked like skeletons.

It wasn't until the early 1980s, when a couple of travelers from upstate Vermont visited Europe and saw the modern version of skeleton, that it returned to the United States. For years, though, even the most basic information—like how to steer—remained a mystery.

"When we started, we provided comic relief for the Europeans," says Terry Holland, a coach of the U.S. Olympic team, who began sliding in 1982. "For all the violence, it really is a **subtle** sport."

DeWitt acknowledges that he went through his entire first year on the skeleton circuit without really knowing how to **maneuver** his sled. "Whenever you saw someone who knew something about skeleton, you'd ask, 'How do you make the sled do this, or turn to the right?'" he says.

Now, after experimentation and interrogation, such knowledge is more widespread: Sleds can be guided with pressure applied by the shoulders or thighs, as well as by dragging the feet—though that is a last resort, since it slows the slider down.

"We can teach someone something in three weeks that took us three years to figure out," adds Holland.

Talking About the Story

Have students tell what they learned from this article.

Ask students to describe what they like or don't like about the sport, skeleton. Would they like to try it? Why or why not?

Vocabulary in Action

Words From the Story

skim

An athlete describes how skeleton is similar to sticking your head out of a fast moving car so that it almost skims the road. If something skims over something else, it moves very quickly along the top of it.

- Ask which would more easily skim the surface of a lake, a boat or an elephant. Explain.
- Have students skim their hands over their desk tops.

insistent

In the story, Tristan Gale is insistent about the excitement of skeleton. If you say something in an insistent way, you keep telling people that it is so, even if they disagree.

- Ask who is more insistent, a dog sleeping under the dinner table or a dog standing by your chair begging for food. Why?
- Ask students to say "we should go fly kites now" in an insistent tone of voice.

unscathed

When U.S. athletes were just learning skeleton, athletes were happy just to complete a skeleton run unscathed. If you are unscathed after something dangerous happens, you have not been hurt by it.

- Ask students who is unscathed, the girl who tripped and scraped her knees or the girl who tripped but was perfectly fine. Explain your answer.
- Have students give examples of dangerous situations and how they might escape them unscathed.

subtle

In the story, Terry Holland describes skeleton as a subtle sport because there's no obvious way to steer. If something is subtle, you may not notice it right away because it doesn't stand out.

- Ask students which is subtle, a quiet piece of background music or a thumping drum solo. Why do you think so?
- Have students describe things or people that are subtle.

maneuver

In the story, athletes maneuver their sleds down the track. When you maneuver something, you move it for a particular reason.

- Ask who is maneuvering something, the boy sleeping in a hammock or the boy riding a bike. Why is that?
- Have students take turns acting out ways to maneuver different vehicles.

Vocabulary in Action

Words About the Story

intense

Skeleton is an extremely demanding, dangerous sport that takes all your concentration. In other words it is an intense sport. When something is intense, it is very strong or goes to an extreme degree.

- Ask which has a more intense taste, a jalapeño pepper or a slice of bread. Why do you think so?
- Have students tell about a time when they saw or felt something intense.

audacious

Skeleton athletes are unusually daring. Another way to say that is that they are audacious. An audacious person tries some wild things, even taking risks, to reach their goals.

- Ask students who is more audacious, a stunt person or an office worker. Why?
- Have students say some audacious things they would like to do.

fanatical

Athletes in this story speak of skeleton with great excitement and enthusiasm. You could also say they are fanatical about their sport. Someone is fanatical if they feel so strongly about something that it's almost crazy.

- Ask who is more fanatical, the boy who spends all his time and energy practicing the flute or the boy who has a lot of different interests. Explain your answer.
- Ask students what someone who is fanatical about fashion might do whenever they could.

The Miller's Good Luck

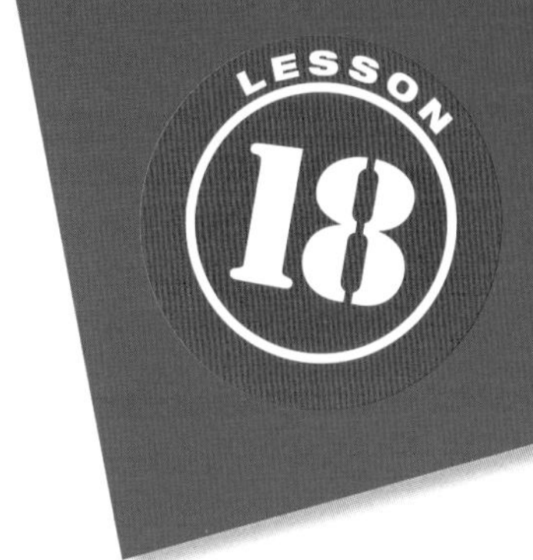

A miller experiences a series of dramatic highs and lows after he meets two rich merchants who attempt to find out what makes a person wealthy.

Vocabulary

Words From the Story

These words appear in blue in the story. Explain these words after the story is read.

prosper **squander**
reputation **flabbergasted**
transpire

Words About the Story

Explain these words after the story is read, using context from the story.

altercation **verify**
speculate

Getting Ready for the Read-Aloud

Show students the picture on pages 142–143 and read the title aloud. Have students notice the people in the picture and their surroundings and then ask them to predict what might happen in the story.

Explain that this story is a folktale. Tell students that folktales are based on the stories passed down within a group of people. Folktales usually tell the traditional beliefs, legends, and customs of a group of people. This story is a Mexican folktale. It is set in New Mexico and is concerned with finding out how a person becomes wealthy.

There are some words and phrases in the story that may be new to students. You might wish to briefly explain these words and phrases as you come to them: *put our theories to a test,* see whether what we believe is correct; *blacksmith/smithy,* someone who shapes metal into parts and objects using heat and a hammer; *mill,* a place where grain is crushed into flour; *pesos,* Mexican money; *not our fate to have fortune,* not supposed to be rich; *lead,* a kind of metal; *"Buenas tardes, vecino,"* "Good evening, neighbor."

GENRE
Mexican Folktale

The Miller's Good Luck

from *My Land Sings: Stories from the Rio Grande*

By Rudolfo Anaya Illustrated by Robert Crawford

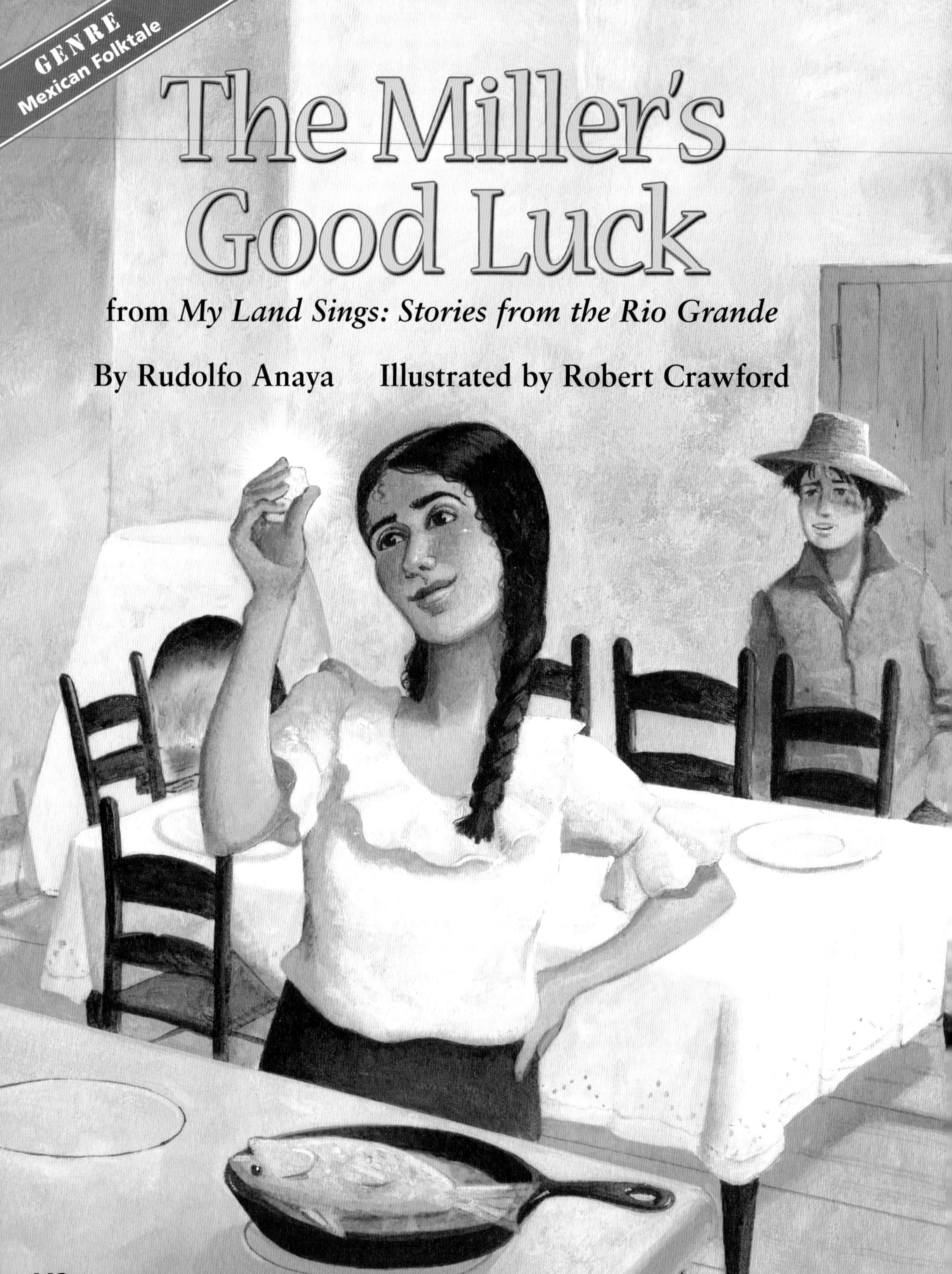

Bringing the Story to Life

Read with enthusiasm, raising your voice when the merchants are arguing and adjusting your tone as is appropriate to Pedro's fluctuating fortunes. Use facial expressions to reflect the emotions of each character as they speak. Also, be sure to emphasize any passages that talk about luck or hard work, as well as any passages that describe the miller as an honest man.

One evening, two rich merchants got into an argument. The two men were arguing about the role of luck in a person's life. Was it luck or careful planning that made the man?

"Luck plays the most important role in a man's life," Libor said.

"No, no!" his friend Vidal answered. "One has to work hard and invest for the future."

"Let's put our theories to a test," Vidal said. "First, let us find a poor but honorable man. We will give him a sum of money to do with as he pleases. Later, we'll check on him and see what he has done with it. That way, we can judge whether the luck of receiving the money makes him **prosper**, or if he remains as he was before."

"Excellent idea," agreed Libor.

What do the rich merchants plan to do?

It so happened that a month later they had to travel together to Santa Fe on business. Near Bernalillo, one of the carts broke down, so they stopped at the blacksmith's shop to have it repaired. While they were waiting, they noticed a small mill near the river.

"Who owns that mill?" Libor asked the smithy.

"Pedro Bernal," the smithy answered. "He is honest, but very poor. He hardly makes enough to feed his family."

The two friends looked at each other.

Together they walked to the miller's shop. "Good friend," Vidal called to the miller. "Are you an honest man?"

"Yes, I am," replied Pedro Bernal. "I value my **reputation** above all things."

"My friend and I would like to put you to a test," said Vidal. "Allow us to give you one hundred pesos. You may do anything you wish with the money."

"Why would you give me a hundred pesos?" asked Pedro, nervous at the very idea. He had never seen that much money in his life.

"It's a bet my friend and I have. We mean no ill will toward you. The money is yours to use any way you want."

Pedro looked at the shiny coins. He needed many things. But he had always been an independent man, and he believed only in what he earned.

"All right," he said, after considering his answer carefully. "I'll take the money."

His hands shook as he received the coins. This is my lucky day, he thought. I didn't earn this, and here it is!

What do you think Pedro will do with the money?

The two merchants said good-bye and went on their way to Santa Fe.

Pedro put the coins in a leather bag and spent the rest of the afternoon wondering what to do with the money.

The first thing I should do is buy food for my family, he thought as he closed his shop. He went to the village store and bought a leg of lamb.

On the way home, he stopped to rest. As Pedro was nodding off, a large hawk circling overhead saw the leg of lamb and dove for it. Pedro jumped up and grabbed the meat. The hawk swerved, seized the bag with the pesos, and flew off with it.

"Oh, poor me," groaned Pedro, "to save the meat, I lost the money. I have no luck. Now I am the same poor miller I have always been."

The hawk flew off with the bag of money! What terrible luck!

A week later, Libor and Vidal were on their way back to Las Cruces. When they came to Bernalillo, they stopped by the miller's place.

"What has **transpired** in your life since we gave you the hundred pesos?" Libor asked.

Pedro hung his head. He was afraid they would think the story of the hawk was a lie, but he told them anyway. He was so persuasive that Libor and Vidal believed him.

"Let's try again," said Vidal.

"I agree." Libor nodded.

"No," pleaded Pedro, "find someone else to give the money to."

"No, no," the two insisted. "You are an honest man. Take these hundred pesos. You may do whatever you desire with the money."

So Pedro took the money and the two men drove away, promising to see him in a few months.

I don't want to make a mistake this time, thought Pedro. I won't stop anywhere until I get home. He wrapped the coins in a bundle and ran home to tell his wife. She wasn't there when he arrived, so he looked around for a place to hide the money. He found a clay jar filled with wheat in the pantry.

"This wheat has been here a year and no one has used it," he said. "It's a perfect place to hide the money."

He emptied the wheat on the table, placed the bundle at the bottom of the jar, then covered it with the grains.

Is that a good hiding place for the money?

Late that afternoon when he returned home, his wife greeted him at the door with a smile.

"I made an excellent deal today," she said. "Look." She showed him a new tablecloth on the table. "I traded that old jar of wheat we had in the pantry. A traveling salesman took it for the tablecloth."

"Oh no," Pedro groaned. "Who was the man?" he shouted.

"I've never seen him before," replied his surprised wife. "He said he lives near Placitas, but I don't know him."

Pedro told her the story. "You have traded a fortune for a tablecloth that costs a few pesos," he moaned.

"Have faith," his wife said, trying to console him. "Perhaps it's not our fate to have fortune or good luck."

So Pedro was consoled and went back to his work as usual. Months later, the two merchants from Las Cruces came up the dusty road again. They stopped to visit with Pedro, and he told them the entire story.

"I find this hard to believe," Vidal complained to his partner. "Twice he has told us wild stories."

"It's only that luck has been against him," said Libor. "Look around you. He is as poor as he was when we first met him."

"Let's be on our way," Vidal insisted. "I'll **squander** no more money on this poor fellow."

"Very well," Libor agreed, turning to Pedro. "Oh, by the way, here's a worthless piece of lead I've been carrying. May it bring you good luck." He laughed, and the two drove away.

Do you think the piece of lead will bring Pedro luck?

While Pedro and his family were eating supper, his neighbor came by.

"Buenas tardes, vecino. I'm going fishing tomorrow, but I have no lead for my lines. Do you have any you can spare?"

Pedro offered him the lead the merchant had given him and wished his neighbor good luck.

Do you think Pedro just gave away something of value?

"Thank you," the man said. "I promise you that the first fish I catch is yours."

"Think nothing of it," Pedro replied. The next day, he went to work as usual, and when he returned home that afternoon, he found his wife cooking a big fish.

"Where did you get the fish?" asked Pedro.

"Our neighbor brought it to us. Don't you remember? He promised to give us the first fish he caught. You wouldn't believe what I found in the stomach of the fish when I cleaned it," his wife said.

"What?"

"A beautiful piece of glass." She showed him the large piece of glass, which glittered brightly.

What do you think Pedro's wife found?

"Take it to the jeweler," his wife suggested. "Maybe he'll give you a few pesos for it."

The next day, Pedro put the glass in his pocket, and on his way to work, he stopped at the jeweler's shop. Pedro took out the piece of glass and showed it to the jeweler. "How much will you give me for this?"

The jeweler examined the object and nearly choked. It was a priceless diamond.

"Ah," he stammered. "It's pretty glass, but almost worthless. I'll give you five pesos."

Pedro was about to say yes when a fly landed on his nose. "¡Oyé!" he said loudly, swiping at it. The jeweler took Pedro's exclamation to mean no.

"Okay, okay, I'll give you a hundred pesos!" he exclaimed, eager to have the beautiful diamond.

Pedro was **flabbergasted**. Why would the jeweler suddenly increase his price? Ah well, a hundred pesos for a piece of glass was great. He was about to say yes when the same fly landed on his ear.

"Shh!" Pedro exclaimed, and threw up his arms.

The jeweler shrank back. Obviously, Pedro knew the value of the diamond and was very irritated at such a low price.

Wow, Pedro's luck sure seems to have turned around.

"Very well!" he cried. "I'll give you fifty thousand pesos for the diamond!"

Pedro's mouth dropped. Fifty thousand pesos? A diamond? It seemed impossible.

"You joke with me," stammered Pedro.

"No, my friend," said the worried jeweler, thinking he had insulted Pedro. He tried to soothe him. "I would not dream of joking with you. I'll give you seventy-five thousand pesos. That's my last offer."

"Bueno," Pedro replied, quaking in his boots. "I'll take it."

"You drive a tough bargain," the jeweler said, going to his safe for the money. "I have bargained all my life, and I've never met anyone as good as you."

Pedro held the bundle of money in his trembling hands. No one in the village had this much money. He hurried home to tell his wife what had happened.

"What are you going to do with so much money?" she asked.

"I'll invest it in the mill. Make it larger so I can serve more farmers. And we always wanted a summer cottage at the foot of the Sandia Mountains. Now we can build one. What's left, we can put in the bank for our old age."

A year passed, and one day while Pedro was sitting in his office at the mill, the two merchants from Las Cruces drove up.

"My, my," one of the merchants said. "We see you have expanded your mill."

The two men admired the new building, the busy workers, the goodwill that seemed part of the enterprise. Pedro was now an employer who hired many men to work for him.

"You have made many improvements," Vidal said. "How did all this come about?"

Pedro told them the story of the diamond his wife had found in the fish and how he had sold it.

"So it was pure luck that made you wealthy!" Libor exclaimed.

Do you think Pedro's wealth is pure luck?

"Wait a minute!" interjected Vidal. "I just don't believe his story."

"I wish there were some way I could prove what has happened," Pedro said. "But since that's impossible, please stay and have lunch. After we eat, I want to show you my cabin at the foot of the mountain."

The two merchants agreed, and after a wonderful feast, Pedro's servants saddled three of his finest horses. Then the three men, followed by Pedro's servants, rode up the mountain. The merchants admired the cabin. Here was a man who only a year ago had been a poor miller. Now he had the home of a rich man, a thriving business, a wonderful mountain house, many servants, whom he paid well, and money in the bank. How did all this happen?

Later in the afternoon, when they stopped at a stream to enjoy a cool drink, they spied a huge nest on the branch of a tall pine tree.

"What is that?" asked Vidal.

"A hawk's nest," replied Pedro.

"I've never seen one. Let's have a closer look at it."

Pedro ordered one of his servants to climb the tree and bring the nest down for inspection. The servant noticed a tattered bag at the bottom of the nest and pulled it out.

What do you think is in the bag?

"That's the bag the hawk stole from me!" Pedro cried. He eagerly tore at the weathered bag, and, sure enough, out fell the coins.

"You told us the truth," Vidal said. "You are an honest man."

They congratulated the miller.

They rode down to Placitas and stopped to rest their horses. Since they had not brought wheat or bran for the horses to eat, Pedro sent one of his servants to buy grain at the home of a man who used to be a traveling salesman. The servant quickly returned with a clay jar of wheat.

What do you think they will find in the clay jar?

"It's old wheat," said the servant, "but it's been well covered. The horses will eat it."

When he emptied the clay jar to feed the horses, out dropped a bundle.

Pedro, who immediately recognized the jar, took the bundle. "This is the same clay jar in which I hid the second hundred pesos you gave me," he told the merchants.

"Let's have a look at it," said Libor. He tore the rags open and out fell the money. "You told us the truth about this incident, too, for here is the money," he said.

They praised Pedro. He was truly an honest man. Now they believed his story of the diamond his wife had found in the fish. But they still couldn't decide if it was luck or planning ahead that had made the miller a wealthy man.

Talking About the Story

Have students summarize the story to tell how Pedro became a wealthy man.

Ask students if it is luck or planning ahead that makes a person wealthy.

Vocabulary in Action

Words From the Story

prosper

In the story, Vidal states that he would like to see whether or not the luck of receiving money will make someone prosper. If someone prospers, they are successful and do very well.

- Ask students who is prospering, the owners of a restaurant where everyone eats dinner or someone who barely has the money to eat dinner. Why?
- Have students tell about some people they know of who have prospered.

reputation

Pedro states that his reputation as an honest person is very important to him. Your reputation is what you are known for or what other people think of you.

- Ask which person probably has a bad reputation, a girl who cares about animals or a boy that people say acts like an animal. Explain.
- Have students discuss the importance of a good reputation.

transpire

After some time, the two merchants ask the miller what has transpired since they gave him the bag of money. When something transpires a certain way, it happens or develops that way.

- Ask where a swimming contest might transpire, in a swimming pool or in a refrigerator. Explain your answer.
- Have students describe what transpired in class before this story was read.

squander

After the miller loses the money for a second time, the merchants agree that they should not squander any more money on him. If you squander money or a chance to do something, you waste it for a foolish reason.

- Ask who is squandering an opportunity to become a dog trainer, someone who is good with animals who goes out and plays or someone who is good with animals who teaches his dog tricks. Explain why.
- Have students talk about a time when they or someone they know squandered their money.

flabbergasted

Pedro is flabbergasted that the jeweler would give him so much money for the "piece of glass." Someone who is flabbergasted is so surprised that they don't know what to think.

- Ask who might be flabbergasted, someone who finds a wolf in their room or someone who is bored of watching TV. Why do you think so?
- Have students practice making facial expressions that show that they are flabbergasted.

Vocabulary in Action

Words About the Story

altercation

The two merchants disagree strongly about how important luck, hard work, and careful planning are to a person's becoming wealthy. Another way to say that is that they have an altercation. An altercation is a noisy argument or disagreement.

- Ask what an altercation looks like, two people talking quietly and agreeing with each other or two people yelling and arguing with each other. Explain why.
- Have students discuss ways that they can avoid altercations with others.

speculate

One merchant predicts that luck makes a person wealthy, and the other merchant predicts that hard work and careful planning make a person wealthy. Another way to say that is that they speculate about what makes a person wealthy. If you speculate about something, you make guesses about what it is or what might happen.

- Ask students what might be speculating, saying that wood comes from trees or saying they think a piece of wood they found is from a pirate ship. Why do you think so?
- Have students speculate what will happen in their lives twenty years from now.

verify

At first, the two merchants have no way of seeing if Pedro's story is true. In other words, they have no way to verify his story. If you verify something, you carefully check to make sure that it is true.

- Ask students what someone should do to verify the date they were born, read and reread the information on their birth certificate or look at the date on an old birthday card of theirs. Why?
- Have students tell how they might verify where they were last night.

The World's Most Traveled Dog

This article tells of the amazing life of Owney, "the mail dog," a stray who became famous for his far-reaching journeys around the world.

Vocabulary

Words From the Story

These words appear in blue in the story. Explain these words after the story is read.

texture **jaunt**
consistent **extravaganza**

Words About the Story

Explain these words after the story is read, using context from the story.

expedition **indomitable**
amiable **vivacious**

Getting Ready for the Read-Aloud

Show students the picture of Owney on pages 154–155 and read the title aloud. Explain that this is a true story and that Owney was the mascot, or animal symbol, of the Railway Mail Service in the late 1800s. Then have students notice Owney's jacket and the many mail tags hanging from it.

Explain to students that in the 1800s and early 1900s, most mail was sent around the country by train, but mail sent overseas had to travel by ship. Mention that all mail needs to be labeled so that postal workers know where to send it.

The following terms occur in the story: *gang-plank,* the ramp leading aboard a ship; *stowaway,* someone who sneaks onto a ship without paying; *wired,* sent a message to; *wanderlust bug,* a strong desire to travel; *stellar fashion,* an outstanding way; *leisurely,* unhurried.

The World's Most Traveled Dog

By Richard Bauman
Illustrated by Raphael Montoliu

In the predawn darkness, the scruffy little dog scurried up the ship's gangplank. But he wasn't a stowaway. On that August morning in 1895, he was beginning a journey as a registered mail package headed for Japan. It wasn't his first adventure traveling with the mail and it wouldn't be his last, but it would be his longest. And when it was over, he would be world-famous.

Owney was a stray who had captured the hearts of postal workers and the public and become the mascot for the Railway Mail Service. Various accounts tell how one day in 1888 Owney had walked into the post office in Albany, New York, and fallen asleep on a mailbag. When he awoke, he apparently decided the post office was his new home.

Bringing the Story to Life

This is an "amazing animal" story and should be read in a tone of awe and fascination. Use dramatic emphasis when reading such lines as "he would be world-famous," "he collected 1,017 different tags," "he met the emperor, who added a tag to Owney's jacket," and "during his lifetime Owney traveled more than 143,000 miles." If possible, point out some of Owney's destinations on a globe or map as you read.

Recognizing that he wasn't likely to leave, the 30 or so postal workers fed him, played with him, and gave him a place to sleep. Owney's favorite bed was a mailbag. It didn't matter if it was folded flat on the floor or stuffed full of mail. He just seemed to like the **texture** and smell of mailbags, or maybe it was the warmth they provided.

How Owney started traveling with the mail in railroad cars isn't clear. The most **consistent** account is that he would ride atop the sacks on the horsedrawn carts that carried the mail from post office to train station. As mailbags were being loaded into the rail car one day, he jumped aboard unnoticed. He was missed only after the train was long gone. Thus Owney's first mail car excursion was a 150-mile **jaunt** south to New York City.

I wonder what Owney was thinking on his train ride.

Postal workers in New York City wired the Albany Post Office to say Owney was there and to ask what they should do about him. Albany postal workers replied: Mail him back to Albany. Once Owney returned home, someone at the post office realized he might take off again. And so Owney was given a leather collar with a tag asking that he be "mailed" back to the Albany Post Office.

The wanderlust bug had seriously infected Owney, and it wasn't long before he took off on another adventure aboard another railroad mail car. For the next nine years he would travel throughout the United States and do it all "by mail." Between outings he would return to his friends at the Albany Post Office. Nonetheless, he went from being the "property" of the Albany Post Office to the "property" of postal workers everywhere.

The label on Owney's collar asked for mail tags to mark his travels, and this request was honored in stellar fashion. In all, he collected 1,017 different tags from friends and post offices in the U.S. and other countries, too. Those tags are a pretty good record of his travels, and most of them still survive and validate his visits to such cities as Denver, Atlanta, Chicago, St. Louis, San Francisco, Nashville, Baltimore, Grand Rapids, Los Angeles, Milwaukee, El Paso, and Rock Island. He visited smaller localities such as Paris, Kentucky; Puyallup, Washington; and Bald Knob, Arkansas.

Can you believe a dog went to so many different places? Have you been to that many places?

Some of Owney's tokens were coinlike items rather than postal tags. One was good for a free cigar or one drink at a local watering hole in Reno, Nevada. A baker gave him a token good for a loaf of bread. A grocer in Nashville, Tennessee, gave him another token redeemable for a quart of milk.

U.S. Postmaster General John Wanamaker sent Owney a special jacket to carry his tags, but even that was inadequate to hold his collection. Periodically tags were removed and kept at the Albany Post Office.

Most postal workers welcomed Owney in the railroad mail car. He kept them company as they sorted mail while traveling from town to town. Besides liking the little brown mutt, the railroad postal workers perceived him as a good-luck charm. In the late 1800s there were about 400 train wrecks each year, but not one of the trains Owney rode on was ever involved in an accident.

On that August day in 1895 when Owney arrived in Tacoma, Washington, he was traveling "first class"—that is, he was traveling with the first-class mailbags. But though he arrived in town by train, he left aboard a steamship. It was the beginning of an around-the-world **extravaganza** that would earn Owney the title of the World's Most Traveled Dog.

At four in the morning on 19 August, Owney boarded the steamship *Victoria* along with 24 sacks of mail. His friends in Albany had provided him with a tiny suitcase that contained a sleeping blanket (even though he preferred mailbags), along with a comb and a brush so he could always look his finest.

He was sent registered mail as a "Registered Dog Package." It assured he would receive special care on the Washington to Japan leg of his journey.

Owney was well received in Japan. One report states he met the emperor, who added a tag to Owney's jacket. Another report says a representative of the emperor greeted him.

In either event, it's known that the Japanese issued Owney an official passport cautioning him against driving wagons too fast on narrow roads and refraining from writing on the walls of public buildings. From Japan, he sailed to Shanghai and then to Foochow, China.

What did the Japanese passport caution him not to do? Those are pretty silly warnings to give to a dog, aren't they?

In Foochow he was entertained aboard the United States Navy cruiser *Detroit* and given a ribbon by the ship's officers. He continued westward, collecting medals and tags along the way. From Singapore he sailed across the Indian Ocean to Perim at the mouth of the Red Sea, and through the Suez Canal. He stopped briefly at the Mediterranean port of Algiers and at São Miguel in the Azores.

The steamer *Port Phillip* carried him across the Atlantic to the U.S. He arrived in New York, his home state, on 24 December 1895. But his travels weren't over. He was whisked to Tacoma, Washington, aboard a Northern Pacific train. He traveled by mail car, of course. The train pulled into the Tacoma station five days later. It was the end of a 132-day adventure, and Owney was apparently none the worse for the trip.

Owney was no youngster when he circled the globe in 1895, and days of leisurely retirement should have been his reward. But it didn't turn out that way. How do you stop a born traveler from traveling?

He boarded a train to Toledo, Ohio, in late spring 1897. Although no one knew it at the time, it was to be his last journey. In Toledo on 11 June, Owney died, but to this day no one knows exactly how.

A life-size likeness of Owney was donated to the Post Office Department's museum in Washington, D.C. Today Owney, complete with tags and medals, is in a glass case in the Smithsonian Institution's National Postal Museum.

It is estimated that during his lifetime Owney traveled more than 143,000 miles, most of it in railroad mail cars.

Talking About the Story

Have students talk about the most interesting thing that happened on Owney's journeys and what they liked about it.

Ask students if they would like to travel around the world someday. Why or why not?

Vocabulary in Action

Words From the Story

texture

In the story, Owney seemed to like the texture of the mailbags. The texture of something is the way it feels when you touch it.

- Ask what word might describe texture, purple or prickly. Explain.
- Have students touch something at their desk and describe its texture.

consistent

The most consistent explanation of how Owney first got onto a train is that he rode on top of sacks of mail in horse-drawn carts that were going to the train station. Things that are consistent act, happen, or look about the same each time.

- Ask what students might do consistently, brush their teeth or go to the moon. Why do you think so?
- Have students describe something that is consistent in their lives.

jaunt

Owney went on a 150-mile jaunt to New York City. A jaunt is a short trip that you go on for fun.

- Ask students which is a jaunt, a long drive to the home of your mean aunt or a quick drive to the mountains for an exciting hike. Explain your answer.
- Have students tell about a jaunt they went on or would like to go on.

extravaganza

The author describes Owney's trip around the world as an extravaganza. If something is an extravaganza, it is extremely fantastic and amazing.

- Ask students which is an extravaganza, a huge dining room with dancing and many different kinds of food or breakfast at the kitchen table. Why?
- Have students tell about something they have seen or heard about that was an extravaganza.

Vocabulary in Action

Words About the Story

expedition

In 1895, Owney was sent on a steamship to travel around the world. In other words, Owney was sent on an expedition. If you go on an expedition, you take an important trip to reach a particular goal.

- Ask students which is an expedition, going downstairs to the basement or flying to the South Pole to research penguins. Explain.
- Have students describe an expedition they would like to go on.

amiable

The postal workers liked having Owney around, and it was easy for him to make friends with people everywhere. In other words, Owney was amiable. If you are amiable, you are friendly and people like being around you.

- Ask students who is amiable, someone who smiles at people and makes them laugh or someone who yells at people and shakes their fist at them. Why?
- Have students practice being amiable.

indomitable

In the story, Owney traveled for 132 days straight, and he never thought of quitting. Another way to say that is that Owney was indomitable. Someone who is indomitable never gives up or admits defeat.

- Ask who is indomitable, a boxer who gets up no matter how many times he is knocked down or a hamster that stops running on its wheel after a minute. Explain your answer.
- Have students tell about someone they think is indomitable.

vivacious

Even as an older dog, Owney always seemed to be full of life. In other words, Owney was vivacious. If you are vivacious, you are lively and exciting.

- Ask who is vivacious, a person always telling jokes and pulling pranks or a person laying in bed with a cold. Why do you think so?
- Have students show how vivacious they are by using body language.

A Mystery in the Prinzel Home

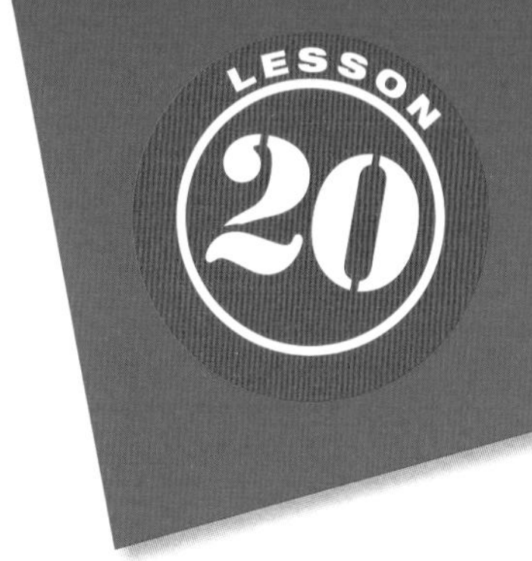

When money starts disappearing from the Prinzel home, the family hatches a clever plan to catch the thief.

Vocabulary

Words From the Story

These words appear in blue in the story. Explain these words after the story is read.

mischief **undeterred**
recruit **meander**
nonchalant

Words About the Story

Explain these words after the story is read, using context from the story.

apprehension **hunch**
sleuth

Getting Ready for the Read-Aloud

Show students the picture on page 162 and read the title aloud. Explain that it shows a girl and her aunt waiting for someone to come into the bedroom. Have them notice the worried expressions on their faces.

Explain that this is a true story that took place in the 1930s. Then tell students that it is about a mysterious robbery. Ask students to talk about right and wrong, specifically, about how stealing is wrong.

There are some phrases in the story that may be new to students. You might wish to briefly explain these phrases as you come to them: *prone to pilfering,* likely to steal; *staking out,* watching very closely; *caught red-handed,* caught while doing something wrong.

GENRE
Nonfiction Narrative

A Mystery in the Prinzel Home

By Mildred Lindsey

Illustrated by Steve Cieslawski

Bringing the Story to Life

Read the story in a lighthearted way until it says, "the store was burglarized." Then increase the urgency in your voice and slow your reading to elevate the suspense. Once the narrator and Aunt Mary Lou have hidden in the closet, soften your voice a bit, as though you're afraid the thief might hear you. Read the final paragraph in a way that is introspective, yet self-assured.

The home of my grandparents, Ma and Pa Prinzel, was always a great place for an adventure. Their house was a well-built wooden structure with just enough windows and rooms to allow for a little bit of **mischief**.

Pa was the postmaster at the small country store located in the very heart of the small town we lived in. He kept the post office cash in a safe until one night when the store was burglarized. The safe was taken and blown up, then left on the side of the highway, where it didn't do Pa much good and couldn't keep anything safe.

After that, Pa began taking all the cash and receipts to his house each night, since it was very close to the store. Pa kept all of that money in the living room, where he naturally assumed it would be safe, as the living room of the Prinzel house didn't normally see much activity.

However, Pa soon noticed that some of the cash he left in the living room was gone. Not one to stand for thievery, Pa came up with a plan to catch the culprit.

He began by putting the cash and receipts in a bedroom that was connected to the back porch. The back porch, an addition to the house, had a closet with a secret window in it that allowed you to see right into this bedroom. This was essential to Pa's plan.

What do you think the plan is?

My Aunt Mary Lou took over the plan from that point on. Quickly dismissing the idea that anyone in the family could have committed the crime, Aunt Mary Lou **recruited** my cousins and me to help her discover the thief's identity.

After a few days of observation, Aunt Mary Lou realized that the Prinzels' next-door neighbor, Eddie, was frequently in the house. He had been hired to help Ma with various chores. So Aunt Mary Lou got organized, planning a trap for Eddie, in order to discover if he was prone to pilfering. Each day, Aunt Mary Lou recruited a different one of Ma and Pa's grandchildren. The chosen child of the day had to arrive at the Prinzel home early and stay inside, so that Eddie wouldn't be aware of our presence. The plan called for the helper of the day and Aunt Mary Lou to enter the closet on the porch and watch through the secret window as Eddie approached the Prinzel house.

The day it was my turn to hide in the closet, I was dreading it. Though my job was simple, it was nerve-wracking: I knew Eddie. He was a little bit older than me and came from a large family. I didn't know whether or not I wanted it to be Eddie. Pa needed to know who was stealing his money, but I didn't want Eddie to get in trouble.

Ma set the plan in motion at about the time Eddie normally came over to help with the chores, which was, coincidentally, about half an hour after Pa brought home the money from the store. Ma went out the back door, making noises and sounds, talking to her dog and to the cats. It was very obvious that Ma Prinzel was leaving the house.

Ma took her time outside, and in the meantime, Aunt Mary Lou and I saw Eddie leaving his home, very **nonchalantly.**

We scrambled into the porch closet just as we heard someone enter through the front door. Then, very, very quickly, the person entered the hallway and immediately turned into the living room. We listened to him go directly to the chest in the living room, where Pa used to keep the money from the store. It didn't take him long to discover that the booty had been moved, but he was **undeterred**.

A few seconds later, Aunt Mary Lou and I saw Eddie creeping into the bedroom we were so carefully staking out. He opened the door to the cabinet where Pa had placed the money and receipts from the store, and we watched him shove about half of it into his own pocket. He was caught red-handed!

Once our theory was proved correct, it was my job to leave the closet and rush to Eddie's home, where I had to entreat his father to come over to my grandparents' house. Once I accomplished this, I realized how reluctant I was to see the confrontation between Eddie and his father. I spent as long as I could chatting with Eddie's younger sisters just to waste time.

Why do you think the narrator is uncomfortable about seeing a confrontation between Eddie and his father?

A little while later, as I **meandered** back to the Prinzel house, I ran into Eddie and his dad on their way home. I will never forget the look on Eddie's face. It reflected not just sorrow but also shame and repentance. It completely convinced me, both then and now, that Pa and Aunt Mary Lou had done the right thing when they decided to solve our little mystery personally. His father's disappointment was punishment enough for Eddie, and, after our detective work revealed his criminal activities, Eddie started earning his money honestly.

Talking About the Story

Have students explain Pa and Aunt Mary Lou's plan for catching Eddie. Was this a good plan?

Ask students how they felt when Eddie was caught. Why?

Vocabulary in Action

Words From the Story

mischief

In the story, the narrator comments that there were just enough windows and rooms in the Prinzel house to allow for mischief. Mischief is something that irritates or annoys people but doesn't seriously hurt anyone or anything.

- Ask students what might be an example of mischief, refilling salt in the salt shaker or replacing the salt in the salt shaker with sugar. Explain.
- Have students talk about a time when they or a family member made some mischief.

recruit

Aunt Mary Lou recruits her children and the narrator to carry out the plan to catch Eddie. If you recruit people for something you are doing, you convince them to help you do it.

- Ask which is an example of recruitment, asking people to help you build a lemonade stand or building a lemonade stand by yourself. Why do you think so?
- Have students tell about a time when they were recruited to do something.

nonchalant

In the story, Aunt Mary Lou and the narrator see Eddie leaving his home nonchalantly. If someone is nonchalant, they seem calm and don't seem to worry about what happens.

- Ask students what is nonchalant, peering around every corner while walking down the sidewalk or strolling past every corner, not caring what might be there. Why?
- Have students use facial expressions and body language to show they are nonchalant.

undeterred

Eddie is undeterred when he discovers that the money has been moved out of the living room. If you are undeterred, you keep doing something, even when other people try to stop you.

- Ask students what is an example of being undeterred, a girl finishing an art project even though people say they don't like it or a girl quitting a game when people say she is no good. Explain your answer.
- Have students talk about a time that they were undeterred when someone tried to discourage them from doing something.

meander

The narrator meanders back to the Prinzel house after she has finished talking to Eddie's sisters. Someone or something that meanders somewhere moves slowly and not in a straight line.

- Ask who might meander, a boy who is wandering through a crowded store or a boy who is running toward his mother. Explain why.
- Have students demonstrate meandering by walking their fingers along their desks.

Vocabulary in Action

Words About the Story

apprehension

In the story, the narrator fears that Eddie will get in trouble. In other words, she feels apprehension. If you feel apprehension, you are afraid that something bad might happen.

- Ask which person feels apprehension, a girl who doesn't want to sleep because she's afraid a monster will eat her or a girl who goes right to sleep without a worry. Explain your answer.
- Have students use facial expressions and body language to express apprehension.

sleuth

The family acts like a team of detectives. In other words, they are a team of sleuths. A sleuth is someone who solves mysteries or investigates crimes.

- Ask students who is a sleuth, a girl who follows muddy footprints to find out who made them or the person who made the muddy footprints. Why do you think so?
- Have students tell about some sleuths that they have heard or read about.

hunch

In the story, Aunt Mary Lou has an idea that Eddie might be the thief. Another way to say that is that she has a hunch. If you have a hunch about something, you have a strong feeling it is true, even though you don't have any proof.

- Ask who has a hunch, a girl who has no idea why her backpack is missing or a girl who thinks she knows who stole her backpack. Why?
- Have students tell about a time they had a hunch about something.

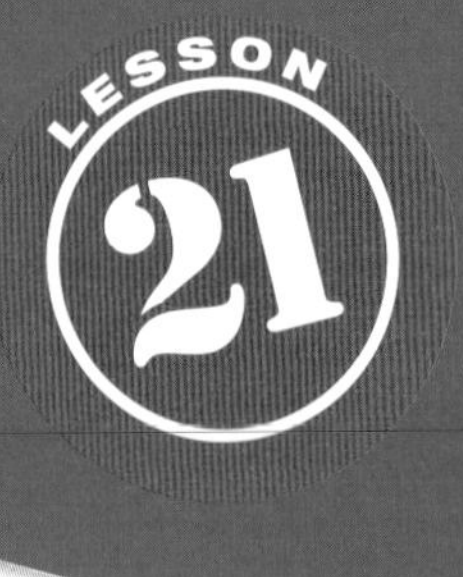

A Family Portrait

Lily and her family take in her Korean cousin, Jung, after Jung's mother dies, giving Lily the sister she always dreamed of having—but it's not quite as simple as that to get a sister.

Vocabulary

Words From the Story

These words appear in blue in the story. Explain these words after the story is read.

fascinate **sashay**
perplex **thwart**
wheeze **distract**

Words About the Story

Explain these words after the story is read, using context from the story.

squat **plethora**

Getting Ready for the Read-Aloud

Show students the picture of Lily and Jung on page 169 and read the title aloud. Have students notice what is different about the two girls and what is similar. Point out that one of them is drawing a picture of a woman. Ask students who they think the woman in the picture is.

Explain that sometimes families are brought together through tragedies, such as in this story, through the death of Jung's mother. In the story, Jung comes to live with her cousin Lily. Because the girls do not know each other and do not speak the same language, it is hard for them to communicate and be friends. Ask students how they might get to know someone who doesn't speak their language.

The following phrases occur in the story and can be explained as necessary: *an angular language,* writing with a lot of sharp angles in it; *her flawless face,* her smooth, clear face; *barbarically,* in a crude, impolite manner; *a burden,* the cause of stress; *the way she carried herself,* the way she walked; *intruding on some sacred rite,* seeing something that wasn't intended to be seen by outsiders.

GENRE
Realistic Fiction

A Family Portrait

By Anna Choi
Illustrated by Matthew Archambault

Bringing the Story to Life

As you read, change your inflection to match Lily's mood: confused to begin with, then excited that Jung was coming, disappointed when things aren't perfect, worried when Jung is missing, and finally happy. Demonstrate phrases that might be unfamiliar to students, such as "like an old horse wheezing and neighing in exhaustion," and "while scrabbling around."

They were sad times when the mother of Lily's cousin died. Lily's mom locked herself in her room when she heard the news and Lily could hear her mother's tears through the door. Lily cried too, but she didn't know why. She had never met her cousin's mother since Lily lived in Texas and her cousin lived in Korea. She simply cried because her mom was crying and she didn't know what else to do. After three tearful days, Lily's mom came and told Lily the most thrilling news: Jung, Lily's cousin, was going to move to Texas and live with their family! Imagine the excitement Lily felt! After daydreaming for so long about having a sister, it was as if her dream was coming true.

Lily had met her cousin only once before and even then it was through a picture. A year before, a package had come in the mail from Seoul, Korea. It was a small brown envelope with hearts drawn all over the front with a pink marker. A bit of rain must have fallen on the package because some of the hearts were blurred.

In it was a picture of her cousin, Jung, and a letter written in an angular language completely unknown to her. Lily's mother had to translate it for her and by now she had forgotten what the letter had said, but she still kept the picture in her desk drawer. She would sometimes pull it out to look at her cousin's perfectly constructed face and imagine that Jung was her long-lost twin. How magical it would be to have a twin sister. After all, they were born in the same month, in the same year. Lily would picture grand adventures of them pretending to be each other. They could switch places and trick all the grown-ups. They could invent a secret code and leave hidden messages in secret places. They could build a club in the woods that no one else would know about.

The truth was Jung was not her twin sister. Their birthdays were off by ten days. Plus, they looked completely different. Lily had never seen her in person, but in her picture, Jung looked like a perfect china doll. Her ruby red lips smiled from an ivory face surrounded by long, sleek hair. Lily, on the other hand, had a dark complexion, tanned by the Texas sun. She was short and stumpy, with thick legs and ankles. She hated her ankles and never wore shorts to school. Jung looked so tall in her school uniform and had long ivory legs beneath her pleated skirt. Lily was proud to have such a beautiful cousin.

How are Lily and Jung alike? How are they different?

And when Jung finally arrived, it was just as wonderful as she had expected. At least, it was at first. Jung was so tall and beautiful, just as Lily had imagined, and she would sometimes catch herself staring at her, **fascinated** by her flawless face. Not only was she beautiful, but she brought along with her an overabundance of beautiful clothes. Lily loved going through the many boxes laid across their bedroom floor. Each box was like a treasure chest filled with shirts that sparkled and skirts with fringe and frills. While Jung was in the shower or downstairs talking with her mother, Lily would sneak away to steal another look at the lovely outfits.

Sure, it was nice at first, but within a week, Lily found herself getting annoyed. It was all just little things, but a lot of little, petty things, when piled on top of each other, can turn into one amazingly colossal thing.

First of all, there was the snoring. Lily had to share her room with Jung because they didn't have a spare room. Jung said she liked to sleep on the ground, so she slept in a sleeping bag beside her bed. Everything was fine on nights when Lily fell asleep first. But when Jung fell asleep first, everything was definitely *not* fine. Exhausted from trying to sleep, Lily would sit up and stare at Jung snoring away so barbarically.

She couldn't explain it. Lily was **perplexed**—how could such a beautiful face produce such a horrendous noise? It started off as a soft whistling and slowly got louder and louder until it sounded more like an old horse **wheezing** and neighing in exhaustion. Lily wanted so much to throw a pillow over Jung's face or at least stuff tissues into her nose. But remembering that she had just lost her mother and moved to a foreign place, Lily merely sighed and stuffed tissues into her own ears and slept with the pillow over her head.

Why doesn't Lily complain about Jung's snoring?

There was also the problem of space. Although Lily admired Jung's clothes, they slowly became a burden. The four large boxes scattered around her room left it cramped with only a narrow path to walk in. With Jung sleeping on the ground at night, it was impossible to leave without stepping on someone's beautiful, snoring face or someone's beautiful, sparkling clothes.

It would have been easier if they could communicate, but with Jung's limited English and Lily's limited Korean, they never got far beyond "Good morning," "How are you?" and "Good night." Besides, Lily never knew what to talk about. Jung always seemed sad and off in some other world. She never even smiled. Well, she would smile from time to time out of politeness or to say thank you, or to hide something. But you never saw a *real* smile on her face—the kind of smile you get when you're happy and laughing on the inside—the kind of smile she had in the photograph.

How does not being able to communicate affect Lily's relationship with Jung?

Most of all, Lily felt disappointed. This was nothing like what she had hoped for: after nearly two and a half weeks, they had done nothing fun together. There were no late-night chats, no club houses, no secret messages—not even a word.

The silence between them kept growing and growing, creating a wall of air so thick it felt as if it was choking her.

Lily wanted so much to understand Jung's world. She knew that there was so much more going on under the surface of her soft eyes and quiet presence. Lily could tell by the way she carried herself, **sashaying** across the room with her head raised high, Jung was trying too hard to appear untouched and strong. Lily imagined what it would feel like to lose her mom and knew that there had to be much more pain beneath those proud shoulders. But Lily didn't know what to do about it. She wanted to talk and ask her how she was feeling, but she didn't think that Jung wanted to share.

She tried many times to approach Jung with a smile and a new suggestion: "Want to watch TV?" "Do you want to try out my new rollerblades?" "Want to go to the park?" In her broken English Jung would politely reply: No, she didn't want to watch TV; she couldn't understand what they were saying because they talked too fast. And no, she doesn't know how to rollerblade. And no, she would not like to learn because what if she fell and scraped herself? And no, she wasn't in the mood for the park. Every attempt was **thwarted** by one excuse or another; the answer was always no.

Lily's mom advised her to just give it time. "Right now the best thing for Jung is time and space." So that's what Lily tried to do—give her time and space. She watched her from afar, watched her while she sat in empty corners scribbling in her little sketchbook. She watched and waited.

Then it happened. One day Lily looked up from her afternoon cartoons and found that Jung wasn't in her usual corner. She called out for her mom but no answer. Her mom must have just run to the store, and maybe Jung went with her. But no, Jung is never in the mood to go the store. Where could she be? Lily turned off the TV and called out, "Jung? Jung?"

Only echoes replied back. Lily stood up and searched the whole house for Jung but she was nowhere to be found. Jung never left anywhere without telling someone. Even if she was just going to go upstairs, she always politely informed everyone where she would be. Worried thoughts crept into Lily's mind.

Maybe she went for a walk or to the park. Maybe she got lost outside. Maybe she got kidnapped! True, Jung did annoy her from time to time, and yes, she snores and doesn't like to smile or talk, but still—she was her cousin, and the closest thing to a sister Lily had ever had. She didn't want to lose her.

Where do you think Jung went? Why does it matter to Lily?

Lily decided it might help to go outside and look and even if it didn't help, anything was better than sitting on the couch imagining all the horrible things that could have happened. She pulled on her shoes and rushed to the backyard to grab her bike. Just as she stepped out into the yard, she heard a noise coming from the other side of the fence. It was a scraping sound accompanied by soft sniffling noises. Lily crept over to the fence and cautiously opened the gate. Peeking her head through the gate, she found none other than the lost Jung.

Crouching on the driveway floor sat her beautiful cousin. She was drawing on the concrete with a piece of broken wood. Hearing Lily she looked up, eyes brimming with tears. Lily felt as if she were intruding on some sacred rite and immediately apologized.

"I'm...I'm sorry. I didn't know where you were and got worried and thought you might be out at the..."

"It's okay," Jung interrupted.

She didn't seem at all mad that Lily had **distracted** her from her drawing.

"Do you want me to leave? 'Cause, I mean, I can go if you want."

"It's okay," she smiled her polite smile.

Smiling back, Lily sighed, "Okay." She crouched down beside her cousin to watch her draw. It was a picture of a beautiful woman, standing like a queen, majestic yet soft, captivating. With the end of a rotting branch Jung was darkening the insides of her eyes, making them darker with every stroke. *Scratch. Scratch.* Lily had never realized what a talented artist Jung was. She had drawn this woman so perfectly, black lines sure and strong against the ivory backdrop of the concrete driveway. As beautiful as the drawing was there was something about it that felt wrong, something missing. The woman seemed to be empty, and even though she was smiling, the woman's eyes looked sad and dim.

If only there was some color. Some color! That's just what this woman needed. Lily got up and rummaged around in the alley until she found some white rocks that were brittle enough to act as chalk. Then in the grass she found some sand stones that left streaks of burnt orange when rubbed against the concrete. While scrabbling around she stepped on some tiny berries and examining her shoes she discovered that they left juicy red stains. Picking up these little treasures she hurried back to Jung and laid them down at her feet.

How does Lily help Jung?

Surprised, Jung examined Lily's gifts with curiosity. Grinning with excitement, Lily placed a red berry in her hand and pointed at the woman's pale lips. Jung seemed to understand this gesture and picking up a berry, she gently caressed the woman's lips with it until the colors bled into the concrete floor. One simple blur of red brought the woman to life and her smile glowed with energy. Jung looked up at Lily with glistening eyes and a smile upon her lips. Some of the woman's life must have transferred into her own lips because this smile was different from all the ones she'd seen in the past—it was a *real* smile, a smile from the inside. Jung took up the white stones with excitement and handed one to Lily. Her smile seemed to say, "Can you help me paint her?"

Together they spread colors upon colors, bringing life to the beautiful woman. Two sisters smiling, eyes laughing, knees bent, hands stained with colors, painting her—the lost mother, now found.

Talking About the Story

Have students summarize what happened in the story and then compare it to a similar experience that they might have had or read about.

Ask students to describe what they liked or did not like about Lily and Jung.

Vocabulary in Action

Words From the Story

fascinate

Lily is fascinated by Jung's beautiful face. If something fascinates you, it interests you so much that you think about it a lot.

- Ask who finds tigers fascinating, the boy who likes to watch movies and read books about them or the boy who barely knows that they're cats. Explain.
- Ask students to describe an event or object that fascinates them.

perplex

Lily is perplexed by how her beautiful cousin can snore so loudly. If something perplexes you, it worries or confuses you because you can't figure it out.

- Ask who might be perplexed, the boy watching a movie in a language he doesn't understand or the boy watching his favorite movie for the third time. Why?
- Have students make a perplexed face.

wheeze

In the story, Jung wheezes when she sleeps. If someone wheezes, they have a hard time breathing and make a whistling sound when they breathe.

- Ask students when they might wheeze, when they have a bad cold or when they are eating dinner. Explain your answer.
- Have students take turns wheezing.

sashay

In the story, Jung sashays across the room with her head held high. Someone who sashays walks in a fancy way that they want other people to notice.

- Ask who is sashaying, the girl who is showing off a new skirt by making it swirl around her as she walks across the room or the girl who is quietly sneaking out of the room. Why do you think so?
- Call on volunteers to sashay across the room.

thwart

Lily's attempts to get to know Jung better are thwarted by one excuse after another. If something thwarts you or your plans, it stops you from getting what you want.

- Ask students which situation might thwart their attempt to get into a garden, a locked gate or an open gate. Why is that?
- Have students give an example of a time when something thwarted their attempt to do something.

distract

In the story, Lily distracts Jung from her drawing. If something distracts you, it takes your attention away from something else.

- Ask students which would distract them more, a teacher walking through the room or an elephant walking through the room. Why is that?
- Have students give examples of when they've been distracted.

Vocabulary in Action

Words About the Story

squat

In the story, Lily describes herself as being short and stumpy. Another way to say that is that she thinks she's squat. If you say someone or something is squat, you mean that they are short and thick.

- Ask which looks squat, a bulldog or a giraffe. Why do you think so?
- Have students point to things in the room that are squat.

plethora

Jung has many boxes filled with beautiful clothes. You could also say she has a plethora of clothes. A plethora of something is a large amount of it, sometimes more than you want or need.

- Ask students which is a plethora, a folder full of homework assignments or two cookies on a plate. Explain.
- Have students describe a plethora of something. Would this plethora make them happy or sad?

FLYING WITH A PURPOSE

This is an excerpt from a biography about Bessie Coleman, the first African-American pilot. Coleman's efforts helped raise interest in aviation among African Americans.

Vocabulary

Words From the Story

These words appear in blue in the story. Explain these words after the story is read.

effortless **native**
exhibition **coast**

Words About the Story

Explain these words after the story is read, using context from the story.

prowess **bliss**
dissuade **diminutive**

Getting Ready for the Read-Aloud

Show students the picture of Bessie Coleman on page 179 and read the title aloud. Explain that the woman in the picture is Bessie Coleman and that she is standing beside her plane. Then have students notice her flying suit. Tell them that this is how pilots dressed in the 1920s.

Explain to students that this story is from a biography about the first African-American pilot, Bessie Coleman. Then explain that Bessie Coleman lived during a time when African Americans and women were not given the same rights and opportunities as other people. Explain that this made it difficult for them to be successful. In addition, it was rare for the accomplishments of women and African Americans to receive any news coverage.

There are some words and phrases in the story that may be new to students. You might wish to briefly explain these words and phrases as you come to them: *biplane,* old-fashioned airplane with two wings, one above the other; *throttle,* the lever that controls speed; *the Charleston,* a popular dance from the 1920s; *Civil War,* war between northern and southern states in the U.S. from 1861-1865; *skywriting,* words written in the sky using a plane's smoke.

GENRE Biography

FLYING WITH A PURPOSE

from *Bessie Coleman: First Black Woman Pilot*

By Connie Plantz

Bringing the Story to Life

Insert dramatic pauses where appropriate as you read the brief description of Coleman's exhibition in the first paragraph, as well as the more detailed description of it later in the story. As you read, use your hands to demonstrate phrases like: "pulled the throttle in," "loop-the-loop, barrel roll, and figure eight," and "whipped off her goggles and loosened her leather helmet strap."

Flying at sixty miles an hour in a borrowed biplane, Bessie Coleman gradually slowed her speed. The plane began to dive. Dangerously close to the earth, she pulled the throttle in to give the engine more power. Then, **effortlessly**, she flew back toward the clouds. It was June 19, 1925. Thousands of spectators at the old speedway auto racetrack in Houston, Texas, cheered and stomped their feet.

Before Bessie became a pilot, unemployed World War I pilots bought used planes to dazzle audiences with outrageous routines that appeared life-threatening. Amateur stunt performers danced the Charleston on the upper wings of biplanes or dangled from rope ladders.

These stunt pilots went from one county fair to the next, entertaining crowds with their dangerous maneuvers. Some people called them "barnstormers." This was a term used for traveling performers who brought their shows to rural areas. Others called the aviators "flying fools" because of their recklessness. A 1921 *New York Times* editorial illustrated the absurdity of these daredevil tricks. It stated that so many pilots had died in crashes that no one cared anymore. Only their relatives and friends showed any emotion when reports of pilots' deaths were printed in the newspaper.

Bessie Coleman was far from being a flying fool. She was an African-American woman with a goal. An article in the *Houston Post-Dispatch* on June 18, 1925, reported that Coleman was attracting attention all over the country for her efforts to interest African Americans in aviation. Her goal, she told them, was to get African Americans flying. Coleman stressed that African Americans were the only group of people in the world who had not been involved in aviation. The *Houston Post-Dispatch* was written and read by whites. Usually, Coleman's exhibitions were covered only in newspapers read by blacks. The fact that this paper reported Coleman's achievements indicated that she had become an entertainer of interest to all audiences.

Why do you think readers were interested in Bessie?

Bessie Coleman chose June 19 for this **exhibition** of flying because it was an important date in African-American history: Sixty years earlier, on June 19, 1865, Union troops came to Galveston, Texas, and announced the end of the Civil War. The slaves there learned that they were all free. Coleman, herself a **native** Texan, used the annual celebration, called Juneteenth, to interest her people in aviation. Every loop-the-loop, barrel roll, and figure eight showed the audience on the ground that an African American could fly a plane. As Bessie Coleman zipped through the sky, her message was as clear as skywriting: Don't be afraid to take risks. Fly!

As she prepared for her last stunt of the show, Coleman checked the windsock attached to a fence post. Seeing the white fabric blowing westward, she knew the wind was coming from the east. Coleman turned her plane to face into the wind. Then, to give the audience one more thrill, she stopped her loud buzzing engine.

Why might this have given the audience a thrill?

In complete silence, she glided the plane to the ground. The forward motion dragged the plane's tail across the rough field. A brass band played a jazzy tune as Coleman **coasted** to a stop. It was a perfect landing.

Coleman whipped off her goggles and loosened her leather helmet strap. She climbed out of the cockpit onto the lower wing, then jumped to the ground. Her petite figure was fashionably dressed in a tailored flying suit and a leather French officer's jacket. Coleman confidently smiled and waved at the crowd.

The spectators whistled and hooted. They pushed onto the field toward five planes waiting to give them rides. About seventy-five people, mostly women, lined up. They were eager for a turn to climb aboard for a bird's-eye view of Houston.

Why were the people so eager to fly?

It was the first time African Americans in the South had been given the opportunity to fly.

On June 19, 1925, Bessie Coleman accomplished her goal. She demonstrated that an African American could pilot an airplane.

Talking About the Story

Have students tell how people felt about Bessie's flying skills. How did Coleman's achievements affect African Americans?

Ask students to tell about someone that they look up to. What has this person done to help others?

Vocabulary in Action

Words From the Story

effortless

In the story, Bessie did a dive with her plane and then effortlessly flew upward. If something you do is effortless, you do it easily and well.

- Ask which task would seem effortless to a chef, grilling some burgers or flying a plane. Explain why.
- Have students take turns talking about things they can do effortlessly.

exhibition

Bessie Coleman held her flying exhibition on June 19, 1925. An exhibition is an event where either interesting things or a skillful activity is displayed.

- Ask students what might be featured at an exhibition, two ice cubes melting away or two dolphins performing tricks. Why do you think so?
- Have students talk about an exhibition they have been to or heard about.

native

In the story, it says that Bessie Coleman was a native Texan. Someone who is a native of a particular country, state, or region was born and grew up there.

- Ask who is a native of the United States, someone born in the United States or someone born in France. Why?
- Have students tell which states they are natives of.

coast

When Bessie Coleman's plane landed, it coasted to a stop. A vehicle that is coasting keeps going without using any power to move it.

- Ask which could be coasting, a bicycle being pedaled up a hill or a wagon rolling down a hill. Explain.
- Have students let their pencils coast down their sloped hands and onto their desks.

Vocabulary in Action

Words About the Story

prowess

Bessie Coleman was an excellent pilot. In other words, she had prowess as a pilot. Someone's prowess is their great skill at doing something.

- Ask students who has prowess with a bow and arrow, someone who always hits their target or someone who never hits their target. Why do you think so?
- Have students talk about activities at which they have prowess.

dissuade

In the story, the deaths of other stunt pilots did not change Bessie's mind about wanting to perform. Another way to say that is that their deaths did not dissuade her from performing. If you dissuade someone from doing something, you convince them not to do it.

- Ask what you would dissuade a friend from doing, eating a peach that is delicious or petting an angry rhino. Explain why.
- Have students take turns dissuading other students from tapping their feet.

bliss

Flying her plane and performing for the crowd made Bessie extremely happy. Another way to say that is that flying and performing were bliss for her. Bliss is complete happiness.

- Ask who would be in bliss, someone in a library who loves to read or someone in a library who wants to leave. Explain your answer.
- Have students practice looking blissful.

diminutive

Bessie Coleman is described as being petite, or small. You could say that Bessie was diminutive. If you call someone or something diminutive, you mean that they are very small.

- Ask students which is more likely to be diminutive, a wrestler or an elf. Why?
- Have students find an example of something diminutive in the classroom.

The Wise Old Woman

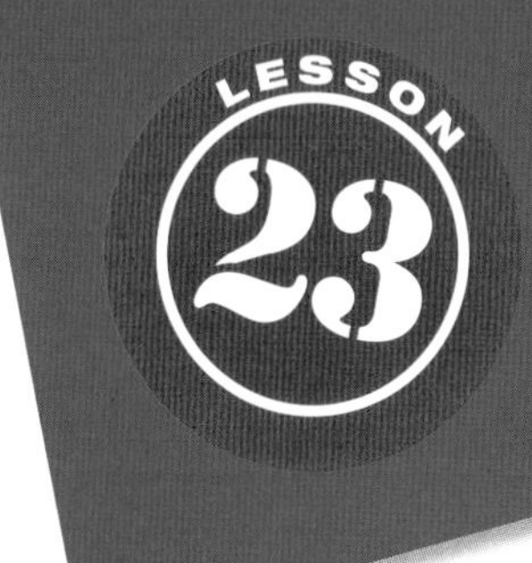

In this Japanese legend, a village is ruled by a cruel lord who announces that old people are useless and must be sent to the mountains to die. One farmer disobeys the law and changes the cruel lord's ideas about the value of the elderly.

Vocabulary

Words From the Story

These words appear in blue in the story. Explain these words after the story is read.

banish
decree
desert
spare
commend

Words About the Story

Explain these words after the story is read, using context from the story.

ruthless
serene
covert

Getting Ready for the Read-Aloud

Show students the picture of the man carrying his aged mother up a mountain on pages 186–187. Read the title aloud. Direct students to study the expressions on the two characters' faces. Ask students why they think the man looks so worried while the old woman looks so calm. Ask students where they think the man is taking the old woman.

Explain that this is a legend that takes place in ancient Japan. In those times, villages were ruled by lords who had a great deal of power. The lords could pass laws demanding whatever they wanted and could cruelly punish anyone who disobeyed them. It was hard for people to go against the laws of these lords, even if the laws were cruel or unfair.

GENRE
Japanese Legend

The Wise Old Woman

Retold by Yoshiko Uchida
Illustrated by Carol Inouye

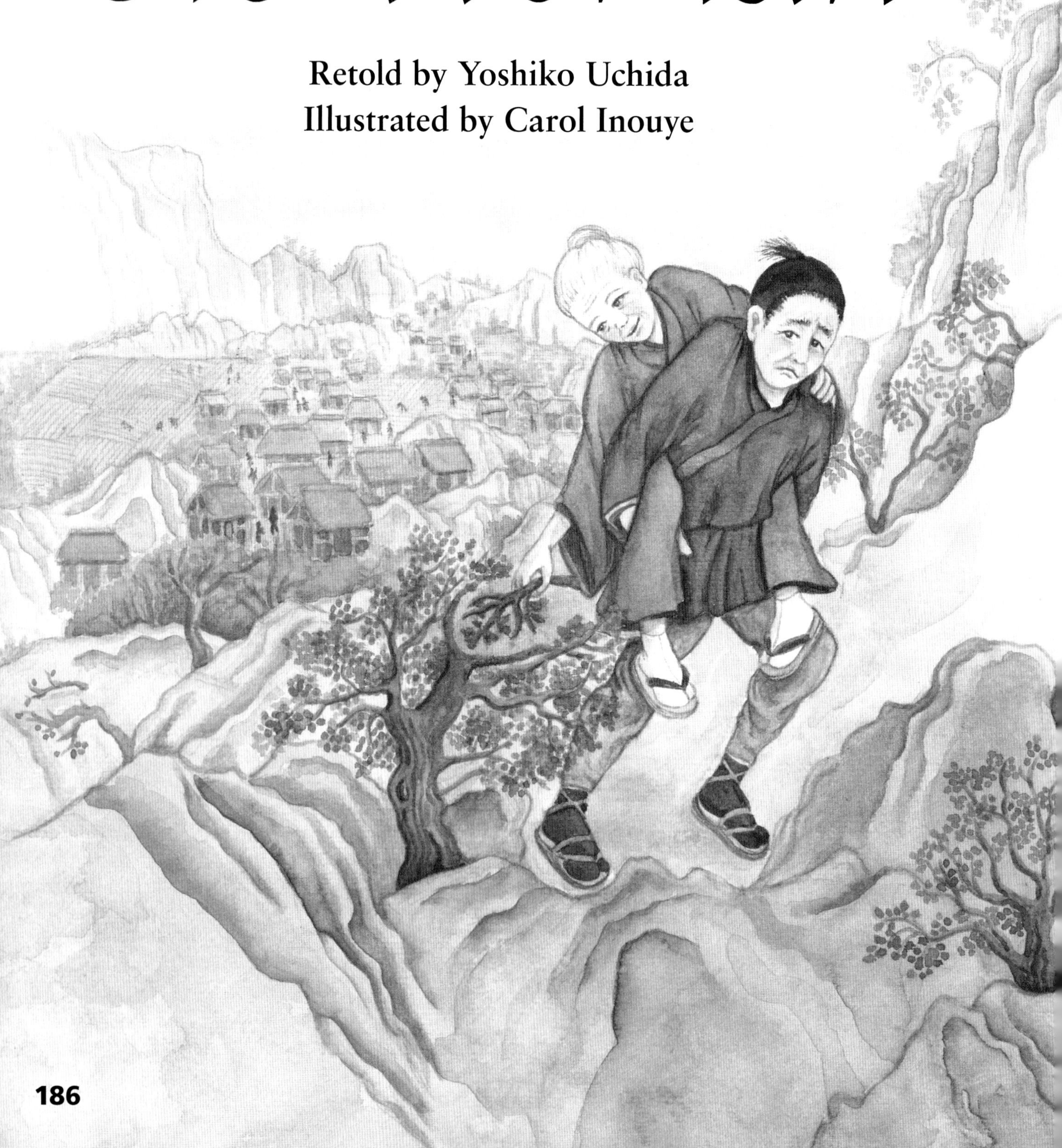

Many long years ago, there lived an arrogant and cruel young lord who ruled over a small village in the western hills of Japan.

"I have no use for old people in my village," he said haughtily. "They are neither useful nor able to work for a living. I therefore decree that anyone over seventy-one must be **banished** from the village and left in the mountains to die."

"What a dreadful **decree**! What a cruel and unreasonable lord we have," the people of the village murmured. But the lord fearfully punished anyone who disobeyed him, and so villagers who turned seventy-one were tearfully carried into the mountains, never to return.

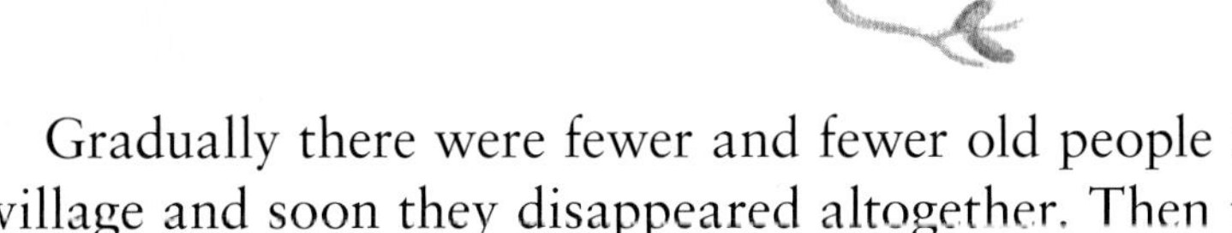

Gradually there were fewer and fewer old people in the village and soon they disappeared altogether. Then the young lord was pleased.

"What a fine village of young, healthy, and hard-working people I have," he bragged. "Soon it will be the finest village in all of Japan."

Now, there lived in this village a kind young farmer and his aged mother. They were poor, but the farmer was good to his mother, and the two of them lived happily together. However, as the years went by, the mother grew older, and before long she reached the terrible age of seventy-one.

"If only I could somehow deceive the cruel lord," the farmer thought. But there were records in the village books and everyone knew that his mother had turned seventy-one.

Bringing the Story to Life

Change your voice to match the characters. The cruel lord changes over the course of the story so start reading his lines with spoiled petulance, but give him more maturity at the end. Give the farmer a meek, gentle voice; the mother a wise, soothing voice, and Lord Higa a booming, angry voice.

What do you think about the young lord's decree?

Each day the son put off telling his mother that he must take her into the mountains to die, but the people of the village began to talk. The farmer knew that if he did not take his mother away soon, the lord would send his soldiers and throw them both into a dark dungeon to die a terrible death.

"Mother—" he would begin, as he tried to tell her what he must do, but he could not go on.

Then one day the mother herself spoke of the lord's dread decree. "Well, my son," she said, "the time has come for you to take me to the mountains. We must hurry before the lord sends his soldiers for you." And she did not seem worried at all that she must go to the mountains to die.

Why do you think the mother is so calm?

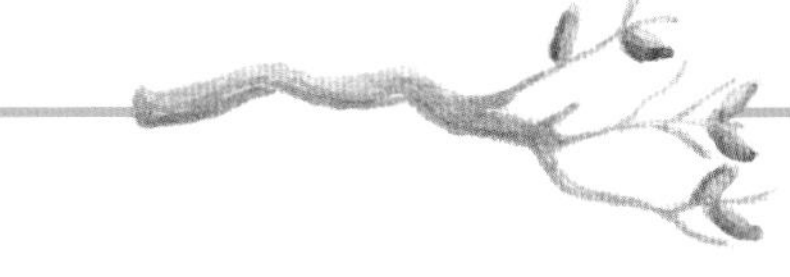

"Forgive me, dear mother, for what I must do," the farmer said sadly, and the next morning he lifted his mother to his shoulders and set off on the steep path toward the mountains. Up and up he climbed, until the trees clustered close and the path was gone. There was no longer even the sound of birds, and they heard only the soft wail of the wind in the trees. The son walked slowly, for he could not bear to think of leaving his old mother in the mountains. On and on he climbed, not wanting to stop and leave her behind. Soon, he heard his mother breaking off small twigs from the trees that they passed.

"Mother, what are you doing?" he asked.

"Do not worry, my son," she answered gently. "I am marking the way so you will not get lost returning to the village."

The son stopped. "Even now you are thinking of me?" he asked, wonderingly.

The mother nodded. "Of course, my son," she replied. "You will always be in my thoughts. How could it be otherwise?"

At that, the young farmer could bear it no longer. "Mother, I cannot leave you in the mountains to die all alone," he said. "We are going home and no matter what the lord does to punish me, I will never **desert** you again."

So they waited until the sun had set and a lone star crept into the silent sky. Then, in the dark shadows of night, the farmer carried his mother down the hill and they returned quietly to their little house. The farmer dug a deep hole in the floor of his kitchen and made a small room where he could hide his mother. From that day, she spent all her time in the secret room and the farmer carried meals to her there. The rest of the time, he was careful to work in the fields and act as though he lived alone. In this way, for almost two years he kept his mother safely hidden and no one in the village knew that she was there.

Then one day there was a terrible commotion among the villagers, for Lord Higa of the town beyond the hills threatened to conquer their village and make it his own.

"Only one thing can **spare** you," Lord Higa announced. "Bring me a box containing one thousand ropes of ash and I will spare your village."

How do you think someone could make a rope of ash?

The cruel young lord quickly gathered together all the wise men of his village. "You are men of wisdom," he said. "Surely you can tell me how to meet Lord Higa's demands so our village can be spared."

But the wise men shook their heads. "It is impossible to make even one rope of ash, sire," they answered. "How can we ever make one thousand?"

"Fools!" the lord cried angrily. "What good is your wisdom if you cannot help me now?"

And he posted a notice in the village square offering a great reward of gold to any villager who could help him save their village.

But all the people in the village whispered, "Surely, it is an impossible thing, for ash crumbles at the touch of the finger. How could anyone ever make a rope of ash?" They shook their heads and sighed, "Alas, alas, we must be conquered by yet another cruel lord."

The young farmer, too, supposed that this must be, and he wondered what would happen to his mother if a new lord even more terrible than their own came to rule over them.

When his mother saw the troubled look on his face, she asked, "Why are you so worried, my son?"

So the farmer told her of the impossible demand made by Lord Higa if the village was to be spared, but his mother did not seem troubled at all. Instead she laughed softly and said, "Why, that is not such an impossible task. All one has to do is soak ordinary rope in salt water and dry it well. When it is burned, it will hold its shape and there is your rope of ash! Tell the villagers to hurry and find one thousand pieces of rope."

The farmer shook his head in amazement. "Mother, you are wonderfully wise," he said, and he rushed to tell the young lord what he must do.

"You are wiser than all the wise men of the village," the lord said when he heard the farmer's solution, and he rewarded him with many pieces of gold. The thousand ropes of ash were quickly made and the village was spared.

In a few days, however, there was another great commotion in the village as Lord Higa sent another threat. This time he sent a log with a small hole that curved and bent seven times through its length, and he demanded that a single piece of silk thread be threaded through the hole. "If you cannot perform this task," the lord threatened, "I shall come to conquer your village."

The young lord hurried once more to his wise men, but they all shook their heads in bewilderment. "A needle cannot bend its way through such curves," they moaned. "Again we are faced with an impossible demand."

"And again you are stupid fools!" the lord said, stamping his foot impatiently. He then posted a second notice in the village square asking the villagers for their help.

Once more the young farmer hurried with the problem to his mother in her secret room.

Do you think the mother will solve this problem?

"Why, that is not so difficult," his mother said with a quick smile. "Put some sugar at one end of the hole. Then tie an ant to a piece of silk thread and put it in at the other end. He will weave his way in and out of the curves to get to the sugar and he will take the silk thread with him."

"Mother, you are remarkable!" the son cried, and he hurried off to the lord with the solution to the second problem.

Once more the lord **commended** the young farmer and rewarded him with many pieces of gold. "You are a brilliant man and you have saved our village again," he said gratefully.

But the lord's troubles were not over even then, for a few days later Lord Higa sent still another demand. "This time you will undoubtedly fail and then I shall conquer your village," he threatened. "Bring me a drum that sounds without being beaten."

"But that is not possible," sighed the people of the village. "How can anyone make a drum sound without beating it?"

This time the wise men held their heads in their hands and moaned, "It is hopeless. It is hopeless. This time Lord Higa will conquer us all."

The young farmer hurried home breathlessly. "Mother, Mother, we must solve another terrible problem or Lord Higa will conquer our village!" And he quickly told his mother about the impossible drum.

How do you think the mother will solve *this* problem?

His mother, however, smiled and answered, "Why, this is the easiest of them all. Make a drum with sides of paper and put a bumblebee inside. As it tries to escape, it will buzz and beat itself against the paper and you will have a drum that sounds without being beaten."

The young farmer was amazed at his mother's wisdom. "You are far wiser than any of the wise men of the village," he said, and he hurried to tell the young lord how to meet Lord Higa's third demand.

When the lord heard the answer, he was greatly impressed. "Surely a young man like you cannot be wiser than all my wise men," he said. "Tell me honestly, who has helped you solve all these difficult problems?"

Do you think the farmer should tell the truth?

The young farmer could not lie. "My lord," he began slowly, "for the past two years I have broken the law of the land. I have kept my aged mother hidden beneath the floor of my house, and it is she who solved each of your problems and saved the village from Lord Higa."

He trembled as he spoke, for he feared the lord's displeasure and rage. Surely now the soldiers would be summoned to throw him into the dark dungeon. But when he glanced fearfully at the lord, he saw that the young ruler was not angry at all. Instead, he was silent and thoughtful, for at last he realized how much wisdom and knowledge old people possess.

"I have been very wrong," he said finally. "And I must ask the forgiveness of your mother and of all my people. Never again will I demand that the old people of our village be sent to the mountains to die. Rather, they will be treated with the respect and honor they deserve and share with us the wisdom of their years."

And so it was. From that day, the villagers were no longer forced to abandon their parents in the mountains, and the village became once more a happy, cheerful place in which to live. The terrible Lord Higa stopped sending his impossible demands and no longer threatened to conquer them, for he too was impressed. "Even in such a small village there is much wisdom," he declared, "and its people should be allowed to live in peace."

And that is exactly what the farmer and his mother and all the people of the village did for all the years thereafter.

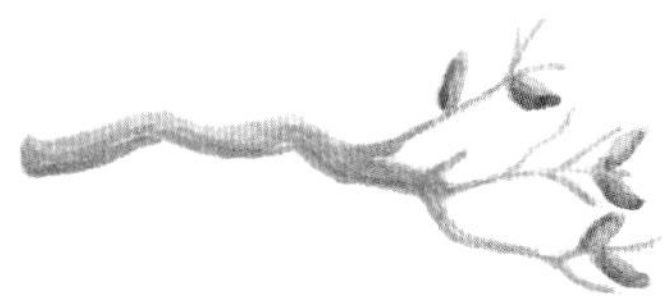

Talking About the Story

Have students summarize what happened in the story. Why is the mother is so wise?

Ask students to describe how they might have met Lord Higa's demands. Can they come up with other ideas that might work?

Vocabulary in Action

Words From the Story

banish

The cruel, young lord banishes all the old people to the mountains to die. If you banish someone from a place, you make them go away and stop them from coming back.

- Ask students who they might try to banish, their own dog or the neighbor's mean dog who fights with their dog. Why?
- Ask students to describe something they would like to banish and explain why.

decree

In the story, a lord issues a cruel decree. A decree is an official order or decision made by a person or group with the authority to do it.

- Ask students who might issue a decree, the president of the United States or their next-door neighbor. Why do you think so?
- Have students take turns pretending to issue decrees on different topics.

desert

The farmer promises to never desert his mother. If you desert someone or something, you leave them and stop supporting or helping them.

- Ask who has been deserted, the boy in the leg cast who's friends have all gone off to play football or the boy in the leg cast who's friends bring him along to cheer from the sidelines. Explain your answer.
- Have students take turns naming objects or places they would be happy to desert.

spare

Lord Higa promises to spare the village if they bring him one thousand ropes of ash. If you spare someone or something, you save them from being hurt or used for something else.

- Ask which has been spared, the old book that is removed from the trash can and kept or the old gum wrapper that is left in the trash can. Explain.
- Have students name items they would spare from being thrown away.

commend

In the story, the young lord commends the farmer for his wise ideas. If someone commends you, they praise you in an official way.

- Ask which person is commended, the one who gets a letter from the mayor thanking them for helping to clean up the city or the one who gets a ticket from the police for littering. Why?
- Have students describe a time they were commended for something they did.

Vocabulary in Action

Words About the Story

ruthless

The lords in the story don't care about anyone else. In other words, the lords are ruthless. Someone who is ruthless is cruel and will do anything to achieve their goals.

- Ask students who is ruthless, a leader who starts a war or a person planting a garden. Why do you think so?
- Have students describe someone they know or have heard about who is ruthless.

serene

In the story, the farmer's mother is always calm and never worried. You could also say she is serene. Someone or something that is serene is calm and quiet.

- Ask students which place is serene, a field full of flowers or a busy city street. Explain your answer.
- Have students give an example of a person who is serene. Why do they think this?

covert

The farmer secretly keeps his mother living with him. Another way to say that is that the farmer acts covertly. A covert action or thing is one that is secret or hidden.

- Ask which is covert, a secret spy mission or a television commercial. Why?
- Have students describe a time when they did something covertly. Why did they act this way?

from The Lion, the Witch and the Wardrobe

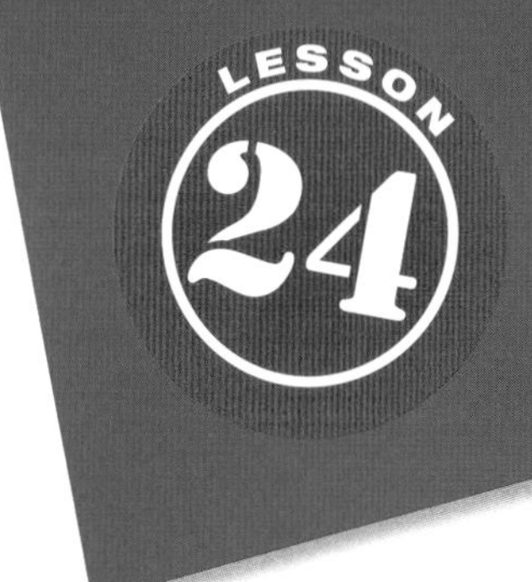

When the youngest of four children tells a story about an entire world hidden inside a wardrobe, the others must decide whether or not to believe her unbelievable story.

Vocabulary

Words From the Story

These words appear in blue in the story. Explain these words after the story is read.

sulk **probable**

jeer **fumble**

consideration

Words About the Story

Explain these words after the story is read, using context from the story.

pretentious **assert**

obscure

Getting Ready for the Read-Aloud

Show students the picture of Lucy on page 196. Read the title aloud. Explain that Lucy is exploring a mysterious forest that she found hidden by a wardrobe, or wooden closet. Ask students if they think a forest like this could fit inside a wardrobe. Point out that in this story things are often different from how they first appear.

Explain that this story is from a full-length book called *The Lion, the Witch and the Wardrobe* by C. S. Lewis. Explain that in the book there is another country on the other side of the door of a wardrobe. Explain that the children have many adventures in the other country but first they must find their way into it.

The following phrases occur in the story and can be briefly explained as you come to them: *a little snigger,* a small, mean laugh; *beastly,* disagreeable or frustrating; *queer,* strange or crazy; *a row,* an argument; *she is mad,* she is crazy; *oh, bother those trippers,* those annoying tourists.

GENRE
Fantasy

from

The Lion, the Witch and the Wardrobe

By C.S. Lewis

Illustrated by Pauline Baynes

Lucy is the youngest of the Pevensie children. She and her older brother Edmund find an amazing wooded land beyond the doors of a wardrobe filled with coats. Lucy bursts out of the wardrobe and enthusiastically tells her other brother and sister about Narnia, the fantasy world within which she had met a Faun. Sometimes stories are too fantastic to believe, and Peter and Susan struggle to understand.

Bringing the Story to Life

When reading the dialogue, use different voices for each character, accentuating the determination of Lucy to stick to her story, the petulance of Edmund, and the worry of Peter and Susan. The Professor is absent-minded but very certain of himself.

Back on this Side of the Door

Lucy burst out:

"Peter! Susan! It's all true. Edmund has seen it too. There is a country you can get to through the wardrobe. Edmund and I both got in. We met one another in there, in the wood. Go on, Edmund; tell them all about it."

"What's all this about, Ed?" said Peter.

And now we come to one of the nastiest things in this story. Up to that moment Edmund had been feeling sick, and **sulky**, and annoyed with Lucy for being right, but he hadn't made up his mind what to do. When Peter suddenly asked him the question he decided all at once to do the meanest and most spiteful thing he could think of. He decided to let Lucy down.

"Tell us, Ed," said Susan.

And Edmund gave a very superior look as if he were far older than Lucy (there was really only a year's difference) and then a little snigger and said, "Oh, yes, Lucy and I have been playing—pretending that all her story about a country in the wardrobe is true. Just for fun, of course. There's nothing there really."

Poor Lucy gave Edmund one look and rushed out of the room.

Why is Lucy upset with Edmund?

Edmund, who was becoming a nastier person every minute, thought that he had scored a great success, and went on at once to say, "There she goes again. What's the matter with her? That's the worst of young kids, they always—"

"Look here," said Peter, turning on him savagely, "shut up! You've been perfectly beastly to Lu ever since she started this nonsense about the wardrobe, and now you go playing games with her about it and setting her off again. I believe you did it simply out of spite."

"But it's all nonsense," said Edmund, very taken aback.

"Of course it's all nonsense," said Peter, "that's just the point. Lu was perfectly all right when we left home, but since we've been down here she seems to be either going queer in the head or else turning into a most frightful liar. But whichever it is, what good do you think you'll do by **jeering** and nagging at her one day and encouraging her the next?"

"I thought—I thought," said Edmund; but he couldn't think of anything to say.

"You didn't think anything at all," said Peter; "it's just spite. You've always liked being beastly to anyone smaller than yourself; we've seen that at school before now."

"Do stop it," said Susan; "it won't make things any better having a row between you two. Let's go and find Lucy."

It was not surprising that when they found Lucy, a good deal later, everyone could see that she had been crying. Nothing they could say to her made any difference. She stuck to her story and said:

"I don't care what you think, and I don't care what you say. You can tell the Professor or you can write to Mother or you can do anything you like. I know I've met a Faun in there and—I wish I'd stayed there and you are all beasts, beasts."

It was an unpleasant evening. Lucy was miserable and Edmund was beginning to feel that his plan wasn't working as well as he had expected. The two older ones were really beginning to think that Lucy was out of her mind. They stood in the passage talking about it in whispers long after she had gone to bed.

The result was the next morning they decided that they really would go and tell the whole thing to the Professor. "He'll write to Father if he thinks there is really something wrong with Lu," said Peter; "it's getting beyond us." So they went and knocked at the study door, and the Professor said "Come in," and got up and found chairs for them and said he was quite at their disposal. Then he sat listening to them with the tips of his fingers pressed together and never interrupting, till they had finished the whole story. After that he said nothing for quite a long time. Then he cleared his throat and said the last thing either of them expected:

What do you think the Professor will say?

"How do you know," he asked, "that your sister's story is not true?"

"Oh, but—" began Susan, and then stopped. Anyone could see from the old man's face that he was perfectly serious. Then Susan pulled herself together and said, "But Edmund said they had only been pretending."

"That is a point," said the Professor, "which certainly deserves **consideration**; very careful consideration. For instance—if you will excuse me for asking the question—does your experience lead you to regard your brother or your sister as the more reliable? I mean, which is the more truthful?"

"That's just the funny thing about it, sir," said Peter. "Up till now, I'd have said Lucy every time."

"And what do you think, my dear?" said the Professor, turning to Susan.

"Well," said Susan, "in general, I'd say the same as Peter, but this couldn't be true—all this about the wood and the Faun."

Why do the others think that Lucy is lying and not Edmund?

"That is more than I know," said the Professor, "and a charge of lying against someone whom you have always found truthful is a very serious thing; a very serious thing indeed."

"We were afraid it mightn't even be lying," said Susan; "we thought there might be something wrong with Lucy."

"Madness, you mean?" said the Professor quite coolly. "Oh, you can make your minds easy about that. One has only to look at her and talk to her to see that she is not mad."

"But then," said Susan, and stopped. She had never dreamed that a grown-up would talk like the Professor and didn't know what to think.

"Logic!" said the Professor half to himself. "Why don't they teach logic at these schools? There are only three possibilities. Either your sister is telling lies, or she is mad, or she is telling the truth. You know she doesn't tell lies and it is obvious that she is not mad. For the moment then and unless further evidence turns up, we must assume that she is telling the truth."

Susan looked at him very hard and was quite sure from the expression on his face that he was not making fun of them.

Why is Susan surprised by the Professor's response?

"But how could it be true, sir?" said Peter.

"Why do you say that?" asked the Professor.

"Well, for one thing," said Peter, "if it was real why doesn't everyone find this country every time they go to the wardrobe? I mean, there was nothing there when we looked; even Lucy didn't pretend there was."

"What has that to do with it?" said the Professor.

"Well, sir, if things are real, they're there all the time."

"Are they?" said the Professor; and Peter did not know quite what to say.

"But there was no time," said Susan. "Lucy had had no time to have gone anywhere, even if there was such a place. She came running after us the very moment we were out of the room. It was less than a minute, and she pretended to have been away for hours."

"That is the very thing that makes her story so likely to be true," said the Professor. "If there really is a door in this house that leads to some other world (and I should warn you that this is a very strange house, and even I know very little about it)—if, I say, she had got into another world, I should not be at all surprised to find that the other world had a separate time of its own; so that however long you stayed there it would never take up any of *our* time. On the other hand, I don't think many girls of her age would invent that idea for themselves. If she had been pretending, she would have hidden for a reasonable time before coming out and telling her story."

How does the Professor explain that Lucy can have so many adventures without any time passing?

"But do you really mean, sir," said Peter, "that there could be other worlds—all over the place, just round the corner—like that?"

"Nothing is more **probable**," said the Professor, taking off his spectacles and beginning to polish them, while he muttered to himself, "I wonder what they *do* teach them at these schools."

"But what are we to do?" said Susan. She felt that the conversation was beginning to get off the point.

"My dear young lady," said the Professor, suddenly looking up with a very sharp expression at both of them, "there is one plan which no one has yet suggested and which is well worth trying."

"What's that?" said Susan.

"We might all try minding our own business," said he. And that was the end of that conversation.

After this things were a good deal better for Lucy. Peter saw to it that Edmund stopped jeering at her, and neither she nor anyone else felt inclined to talk about the wardrobe at all. It had become a rather alarming subject. And so for a time it looked as if all the adventures were coming to an end; but that was not to be.

This house of the Professor's—which even he knew so little about—was so old and famous that people from all over England used to come and ask permission to see over it. It was the sort of house that is mentioned in guide books and even in histories; and well it might be, for all manner of stories were told about it, some of them even stranger than the one I am telling you now. And when parties of sightseers arrived and asked to see the house, the Professor always gave them permission, and Mrs Macready, the housekeeper, showed them round, telling them about the pictures and the armour, and the rare books in the library. Mrs Macready was not fond of children, and did not like to be interrupted when she was telling visitors all the things she knew. She had said to Susan and Peter almost on the first morning (along with a good many other instructions), "And please remember you're to keep out of the way whenever I'm taking a party over the house."

"Just as if any of us would *want* to waste half the morning trailing round with a crowd of strange grown-ups!" said Edmund, and the other three thought the same. That was how the adventures began for the second time.

A few mornings later Peter and Edmund were looking at the suit of armour and wondering if they could take it to bits when the two girls rushed into the room and said, "Look out! Here comes the Macready and a whole gang with her."

"Sharp's the word," said Peter, and all four made off through the door at the far end of the room. But when they had got out into the Green Room and beyond it, into the Library, they suddenly heard voices ahead of them, and realized that Mrs Macready must be bringing her party of sightseers up the back stairs—instead of up the front stairs as they had expected. And after that—whether it was that they lost their heads, or that Mrs Macready was trying to catch them, or that some magic in the house had come to life and was chasing them into Narnia—they seemed to find themselves being followed everywhere, until at last Susan said, "Oh bother those trippers! Here—let's get into the Wardrobe Room till they've passed. No one will follow us in there." But the moment they were inside they heard the voices in the passage—and then someone **fumbling** at the door—and then they saw the handle turning.

What do you think will happen next?

"Quick!" said Peter, "there's nowhere else," and flung open the wardrobe. All four of them bundled inside it and sat there, panting, in the dark. Peter held the door closed but did not shut it; for, of course, he remembered, as every sensible person does, that you should never never shut yourself up in a wardrobe.

Into the Forest

"I wish the Macready would hurry up and take all these people away," said Susan presently, "I'm getting horribly cramped."

"And what a filthy smell of camphor!" said Edmund.

"I expect the pockets of these coats are full of it," said Susan, "to keep away the moths."

"There's something sticking into my back," said Peter.

"And isn't it cold?" said Susan.

"Now that you mention it, it is cold," said Peter, "and hang it all, it's wet too. What's the matter with this place? I'm sitting on something wet. It's getting wetter every minute." He struggled to his feet.

"Let's get out," said Edmund, "they've gone."

"O-o-oh!" said Susan suddenly, and everyone asked her what was the matter.

"I'm sitting against a tree," said Susan, "and look! It's getting light—over there."

"By jove, you're right," said Peter, "and look there—and there. It's trees all round. And this wet stuff is snow. Why, I do believe we've got into Lucy's wood after all."

And now there was no mistaking it and all four children stood blinking in the daylight of a winter day. Behind them were coats hanging on pegs, in front of them were snow-covered trees.

Peter turned at once to Lucy.

"I apologize for not believing you," he said, "I'm sorry. Will you shake hands?"

"Of course," said Lucy, and did.

"And now," said Susan, "what do we do next?"

"Do?" said Peter, "why, go and explore the wood, of course."

Talking About the Story

Have students summarize what happened in the story and tell whether or not they were surprised by the ending.

Invite students to talk about a fantasy world that they might have imagined.

Vocabulary in Action

Words From the Story

sulk

In the story, Edmund sulks because he doesn't like that Lucy is right about the world inside the wardrobe. If you sulk about something, you are quiet and moody for a while because you are annoyed about it.

- Ask who is sulking, the boy who pouts and won't talk because he can't do what he wants or the boy who enjoys doing what he can. Explain.
- Ask students if they have ever sulked about anything.

jeer

Peter tells Edmund to stop jeering at Lucy. If you jeer at someone, you show you don't like them by saying mean things.

- Ask who is jeering, the girl yelling and clapping when her favorite sports team gets on the field or the girl booing when the opposing team gets on the field. Why is that?
- Have students talk about a time when they jeered at someone or when someone jeered at them.

consideration

In the story, the Professor gives careful consideration to the story the children tell him. If you give something consideration, you think about it very carefully.

- Ask students which situation might demand their consideration, what costume to wear to a costume party, or what uniform to wear to a soccer game they're playing. Why?
- Have students talk about a time when they needed to give something consideration.

probable

The Professor says that there's nothing more probable than the possibility of there being other worlds. If something is probable, it is likely to happen or likely to be true.

- Ask which would be more probable, going to school five days a week or going on a year-long vacation? Explain your answer.
- Have students think of some things that are probable.

fumble

The children hear someone fumble at the door when they're trying to hide from Mrs Macready. When you fumble for something, you clumsily try and reach for it or hold it.

- Ask students which might cause them to fumble, carrying five basketballs or carrying five pencils. Why do you think so?
- Have students take turns demonstrating fumbling with a pencil or a book.

Vocabulary in Action

Words About the Story

pretentious

Edmund thinks he is acting important by being mean to Lucy. You could also say that he is pretentious. A pretentious person tries to seem more important than they really are.

- Ask students who is more pretentious, someone who is always trying to explain things even when they don't know anything, or someone who listens to what others have to say. Explain.
- Have students walk across the classroom in a pretentious manner.

obscure

It's not easy for the children in the story to find evidence of the world that Lucy tells them about. You could also say that the other world is obscure. If something is obscure, most people don't know about it or understand it.

- Ask what is more obscure, the capital of the U.S. or a small village in the rain forest. Why do you think so?
- Ask students if they know any obscure facts that other students might not know.

assert

Even though they don't believe her, Lucy tells Peter and Susan about the woods on the other side of the wardrobe. You could say that she asserts that the woods are there. When you assert something, you say it firmly because you're very sure of it.

- Ask who is asserting something, the girl who asks how to get to her friend's house or the girl who answers with the directions. Why?
- Have students talk about a time when they asserted something.

Bibliography

Anaya, Rudolfo. (1999). "The Miller's Good Luck," from *My Land Sings: Stories from the Rio Grande.* Illustrated by Amy Córdova. New York: HarperCollins.

Armstrong, Lance. (2000). *It's Not About the Bike: My Journey Back to Life.* New York: The Berkeley Publishing Group.

Bauman, Richard. (2005). "The World's Most Traveled Dog," from *Cricket*, Vol. 32, No. 8. Peru, IL: Carus Publishing Company.

Choi, Anna. (2005). "A Family Portrait." Austin, TX: Steck-Vaughn.

Current Science. (2003). "Space Rock Barely Misses Sleeping Teen," from *Current Science*, Vol. 89, No. 1. Stamford, CT: Weekly Reader Corp.

De Lange, Flo Ota. (2005). "Home, Sweet Soddie," from *Elements of Literature, Grade 8, Second Course.* Austin, TX: Holt, Rinehart and Winston.

Eliot, T. S. (1982). "Macavity: The Mystery Cat," from *Old Possum's Book of Practical Cats.* Illustrated by Edward Gorey. Orlando, FL: Harcourt Books.

Erickson, John R. (1983). *The Further Adventures of Hank the Cowdog.* Illustrated by Gerald L. Holmes. New York: Puffin Books.

Friedman, Amy. (1995). "The Merchant's Camel," from *The Spectacular Gift and Other Tales from Tell Me a Story.* Illustrated by Jillian H. Gilliland. Kansas City, MO: Andrews McMeel Publishing.

Griffiths, Andy. (2003). "In the Shower with Andy," from *Just Annoying!* Illustrated by Terry Denton. New York: Scholastic.

Guest, Edgar A. (1934). "It Couldn't Be Done," from *Collected Verse.* New York: Buccaneer Books.

Hemingway, Ernest. (1998). "A Day's Wait," from *The Complete Short Stories of Ernest Hemingway.* New York: Scribner.

Hoose, Phillip. (2001). *We Were There, Too!: Young People in U.S. History.* New York: Farrar, Straus and Giroux Publishers.

Johnston, Tony. (1998). *Bigfoot Cinderrrrrella.* Illustrated by James Warhola. New York: Putnam Juvenile.

Kuskin, Karla. (1999). "The Birthday of Madeleine Blore," from *20th Century Children's Poetry Treasury.* Ed. Jack Prelutsky. Illustrated by Meilo So. New York: Random House Children's Books.

Lewis, C. S. (1950). *The Lion, the Witch and the Wardrobe.* Illustrated by Pauline Baynes. London: Collins Publishing Group Children's Division.

Lindsey, Mildred. (2005). "A Mystery in the Prinzel Home." Austin, TX: Steck-Vaughn.

Neill, Michael and Michaele Ballard. (2001). "Helping Hooves," from *People Magazine*, Vol. 55, No. 8. New York: Time Inc.

Pedtke, Ann. (2005). "Comet," from *Cricket*, Vol. 32, No. 5. Peru, IL: Carus Publishing Company.

Plantz, Connie. (2001). *Bessie Coleman: First Black Woman Pilot.* Berkeley Heights, NJ: Enslow Publishers.

Sappenfield, Mark. (2002). "Skeleton, in the flesh, is a real thrill," from *Christian Science Monitor*, Boston: The First Church of Christ, Scientist.

Soto, Gary. (1990). "The Marble Champ," from *Baseball in April and Other Stories.* Orlando, FL: Harcourt Books.

Uchida, Yoshiko. (1965). "The Wise Old Woman," from *Elements of Literature: Second Course.* Austin, TX: Holt, Rinehart and Winston.

Vande Velde, Vivian. (1995). "Mattresses," from *Tales from the Brothers Grimm and the Sisters Weird.* Orlando, FL: Harcourt Books.

Wooldridge, Connie Nordhielm. (2004). "A President's Bumpy Ride," from *Cricket*, Vol. 31, No. 11. Peru, IL: Carus Publishing Company.

Additional Favorite Read-Alouds

Alexander, Lloyd. (1977). *The Town Cats and Other Tales*. Illustrated by Laszlo Kubinyi. New York: Puffin Books.

Broadwater, Andrea. (2000). *Marian Anderson: Singer and Humanitarian*. Berkeley Heights, NJ: Enslow Publishers.

Carroll, Lewis. (1871). *Through the Looking-Glass*. Mineola, NY: Dover Publications.

Dahl, Roald. (1953). *Skin and Other Stories*. New York: Penguin Putnam Books for Young Readers.

Freedman, Russell. (1987). *Lincoln: A Photobiography*. Boston: Houghton Mifflin Company.

Griffith, Helen V. (1987). *Journal of a Teenage Genius*. New York: Harcourt College Publishers.

Pinkney, Andrea Davis. (1998). *Duke Ellington: The Piano Prince and His Orchestra*. Illustrated by Brian Pinkney. New York: Hyperion.

Twain, Mark. (1876). *The Adventures of Tom Sawyer*. Berkeley, CA: University of California Press.

White, E. B. (1952). *Charlotte's Web*. Illustrated by Garth Williams. New York: HarperCollins.